2007

THE BEST 10-MINUTE PLAYS
FOR TWO ACTORS

SMITH AND KRAUS PUBLISHERS
Short Plays and 10-Minute Plays Collections

Christopher Durang Vol. I: 27 Short Plays
Frank D. Gilroy Vol. II: 15 One-Act Plays
Israel Horovitz Vol. I: 16 Short Plays
Romulus Linney 17 Short Plays
Terrence McNally Vol. I: 15 Short Plays
Lanford Wilson: 21 Short Plays
Act One Festival 1995: The Complete One-Act Plays
Act One Festival 1994: The Complete One-Act Plays
EST Marathon 1999: The Complete One-Act Plays
EST Marathon 1998: The Complete One-Act Plays
EST Marathon 1997: The Complete One-Act Plays
EST Marathon 1996: The Complete One-Act Plays
EST Marathon 1995: The Complete One-Act Plays
EST Marathon 1994: The Complete One-Act Plays
Twenty One-Acts from 20 Years at the Humana Festival 1975–1995
Women's Project and Productions Rowing to America & Sixteen Other Short Plays
8 TENS @ 8 Festival: 30 10-Minute Plays from the Santa Cruz Festivals I–VI
30 Ten-Minute Plays from the Actors Theatre of Louisville for 2 Actors
30 Ten-Minute Plays from the Actors Theatre of Louisville for 3 Actors
30 Ten-Minute Plays from the Actors Theatre of Louisville for 4, 5, and 6 Actors
2004: The Best 10-Minute Plays for Two Actors
2004: The Best 10-Minute Plays for Three or More Actors
2005: The Best 10-Minute Plays for Two Actors
2005: The Best 10-Minute Plays for Three or More Actors
2006: The Best 10-Minute Plays for Two Actors
2006: The Best 10-Minute Plays for Three or More Actors

2007
THE BEST 10-MINUTE PLAYS FOR TWO ACTORS

Edited by Lawrence Harbison
Foreword by D. L. Lepidus

CONTEMPORARY PLAYWRIGHT SERIES

A Smith and Kraus Book
Hanover, New Hampshire

Published by Smith and Kraus, Inc.
177 Lyme Road, Hanover, NH 03755
www.SmithandKraus.com / (888) 282-2881

First Edition: April 2008
10 9 8 7 6 5 4 3 2 1

Manufactured in the United States of America
Cover and Text Design by Julia Hill Gignoux, Freedom Hill Design
Cover photo by Luke Dennis
from *Normal* by Jami Brandli, directed by Luke Dennis
with Kevin LeVelle as Robert; Joey DelPonte as Bobby Jr.

ISBN-13 978-1-57525-589-7
ISSN 1550-6754
Library of Congress Control Number: 2008923276

Contents

FOREWORD

The ten-minute play as an accepted dramatic form is a fairly recent development. Some would say that its popularity is a result of our diminished attention spans, which may be partially true; but here's how the genre came to be.

For several years, Actors Theatre of Louisville, under the leadership of Jon Jory, commissioned playwrights to write plays of short duration for performance by its apprentice company. This was a way for the theater to do something to help playwrights, but also it was a way to develop relationships with them, many of which bore fruit over the years as these writers went on to have full-length plays staged in Actors Theater's famed Humana Festival.

Over the years, Actors Theatre built up quite a library of these short plays, all of them in manuscript. An editor for the play publisher Samuel French got the idea that maybe other theaters, actors, and students might be interested in these plays if they were made available to them. He managed to swing a deal for French to publish an anthology of Actors Theatre's best short plays, which they were now calling "ten-minute plays." This anthology was so successful that French has now published six such volumes, and most of the other publishers have followed suit, including Smith and Kraus, as its annual ten-minute play anthologies will attest. Bills of ten-minute plays are now produced regularly — all over the world.

There are some who feel that the ten-minute play ought to be an opportunity for playwrights to experiment — with language, with form, with character, with subject matter. "The best" ten-minute plays are therefore the ones that depart the most from conventional drama. For the purposes of this series, here is how I define "best": that which is most useful to people who will buy this book and produce these plays. Some actors and directors prefer straightforward realism; whereas others go for more abstract, experimental plays. I don't carry a torch for any one style, so I have tried to include in this book examples of realism and, shall we say, "non-realism." I hope you will find herein more than one play that rings your bell. They all rang mine.

Most of the plays in this book are by exciting up-and-comers, such as Bara Swain, Andrew Biss, Michael Golamco, Vanessa David and John Shanahan.

Should you find a play (or plays) in this book that you want to produce, you will find information in the back on who to contact for performance rights.

After seven years of doing these books for Smith and Kraus, I have decided to step aside and have turned over the reins to my old pal Lawrence Harbison, who knows as much about the theater and its plays and playwrights as anyone I know. It has been a very rewarding and very challenging task editing these anthologies; but now it is time to hang up my red pencil. I am retiring to Myrtle Beach, there to become one of those geezers who stands around all day in a kilt, sending foursomes of awful golfers off the first tee. In my free time I won't be reading plays: I'll be taking up bungee jumping, hang gliding, and alligator wrestling. There is life beyond the theater.

D. L. Lepidus
Myrtle Beach, S.C.

PLAYS FOR
ONE MAN
AND
ONE WOMAN

ALL IN A DAY'S WORK

M. LYNDA ROBINSON

First produced at: 8th Annual Boston Theatre Marathon, May 21, 2006 at the Calderwood Pavilion, Boston Center for the Arts. Produced by: Boston Playwrights' Theatre. Sponsored by The West End Theater. Directed by: M. Lynda Robinson. Performed by: He: Peter Berkrot; She: Laura Crook.

CHARACTERS
    HE, male, thirties
    SHE, female, thirties

SCENE
    An office

TIME
    The present

NOTE
    The language is intentionally "stilted/politically incorrect" for a reason that
    becomes clear by end of play.

•   •   •

*Setting: A small, plain but tasteful office. Sturdy desk with comfortable desk
chair. Another plain, but comfortable chair in front of desk. At Rise: A Man
sits behind desk, wearing a corporate suit, holding and reading a report. A
Woman enters wearing a corporate suit. She stands formally at the doorway.*

SHE: You wanted to see me, sir?
HE: Yes.
    (She stands, waits)
HE: *(Continued.)* No need to stand, take a seat.
SHE: Thank you.
    (She sits in chair in front of desk. Pause.)
HE: I read your report.
SHE: Yes?
HE: I'm curious. What did you use for sources?
SHE: Sources? I don't understand your question.
HE: *(Impatiently.)* Sources, sources! You based your conclusions on your source
    material, did you not?
SHE: Yes.
HE: Then, what were they?
SHE: Existing company material, sir.
HE: Existing company material?
SHE: Yes, sir.
HE: Material from our own sources?
SHE: Yes, sir, from our own sources.

HE: Our own computer sources, our own records?

SHE: Yes — and hard copy — annual reports — sources like that.

HE: And where did you find these "sources"?

SHE: Umm, here, sir — in our research library, my personal computer, files in my office left by my predecessor — places like that.

HE: Secured access files??!!

SHE: No, sir, just historical records of the company.

(Slight pause.)

HE: But, from what did you draw your conclusions?

SHE: From that information, sir.

HE: But no one has ever drawn conclusions like your conclusions from that information.

SHE: Oh . . . I wouldn't know that, sir, being new and all.

HE: Ah, hah!! Then your research did not include our previous conclusions!!!

SHE: I did read them, sir, but I came up with my own conclusions.

HE: Your own conclusions?!

SHE: Yes, sir.

HE: You didn't agree with our previous conclusions? You think you have better, smarter conclusions?

SHE: *(Carefully.)* My report reflects what I believe to be my best recommendation, having read all the previous accumulated information . . . sir.

(Pause.)

HE: How long have you worked here?

SHE: Three weeks, sir.

HE: Do you know how long I have worked here?

SHE: No, sir.

HE: Twenty-three years.

(He stands and walks to the front of the desk. We see that he is wearing jeans and sneakers with his jacket and tie.)

Not long by some standards, but certainly longer than your brief accumulation of company time and knowledge. Do you understand me?

SHE: Umm . . . you have been here twenty-two years, eleven months, and one week longer than I have, sir?

(Pause.)

HE: And do you know what the average length of employee time with this company is?

SHE: No, sir.

HE: Eighteen years! This is a company steeped in employee longevity, reeking with experience, teeming with historical data.

SHE: Yes, I have observed that, sir.

HE: This is a company that was founded by young men of intelligence, knowledge, and vision . . .

(Begins to pace.) . . . men who have grown white-haired with the strain of adjusting to a new world full of up-and-coming upstarts — "computer-literate" women and minorities who think they can just walk in here and take our accumulated data, our lifetimes of research, and come up with their own conclusions!!

SHE: Well . . . .

HE: Do you have a husband?

SHE: Yes.

HE: Do you have a family?

SHE: Yes.

HE: And what are they doing all day long? What have they been doing these past three weeks when you have been here selfishly drawing your own conclusions?!

SHE: Well . . . they've . . . I've . . .

HE: You need to re-think your life choices, young lady! This is a tough world, a man's world, a . . . corporate doberman-eat-kitten world. Do you think you can just put on a suit and all of a sudden you're part of that world? Do you think we all owe you a living?! Who do you think you are?! Do you think you . . . .

SHE: (Cutting him off — stands.) All right, all right, enough!! Who do I think I am? Just who do you think you are?! How dare you speak to me as if I was a child, an inferior. I am a completely competent, fully grown, adult woman with degrees, with intelligence, and I am an asset to your company. My conclusions are sound, based on training, experience, and insight, and what's more,

(Faces him.)

they're mine and I'm proud of them. My research is accurate, my conclusions are based in fact, and I am proud to present my report to this company!

(Pause. Now very close — face-to-face with him)

SHE: (Continued.) And I'll have you know, I have a wonderful family who love and support me in my career. I have a husband who believes in me, and trusts that I can achieve anything I set out to accomplish!

(Silence — they are now only inches away from each other. They look each other in the eyes. Long pause.)

HE: Well, your husband is one lucky man.

SHE: Thank you — he's also very handsome.

(He puts his arms around her.)

HE: Is he supportive and alluring?

SHE: He's daring and divine.

HE: And you're sexy and seductive.

SHE: All in a day's work, sir.

> (*They kiss.*)

HE: You're clever and creative.

> (*They kiss more passionately. They fall back onto the desk.*)

SHE: What else?

> (*She gets on top of him.*)

HE: Pretty and powerful.

SHE: (*Kissing his neck.*) Mmmmm. Yes.

HE: Strong.

SHE: (*Sitting up. Running her hands over his chest.*) Oh, yes!

HE: In charge.

SHE: (*She kneels over him, legs around him, lifting her head.*) Yes!!

HE: Mmmm. Good. You can do this.

SHE: (*Raising her arms.*) Yes! I can do it!

HE: You're a tiger.

SHE: (*She is on all fours above him, growling like a tiger, rolling her head.*) Yes, a tiger! Grrrrrrrr!

HE: (*He raises himself to his elbows.*) That's the spirit.

SHE: (*Very high energy.*) Yes! I am ready!

> (*She looks at him. Smiles.*)

> Are you OK?

HE: Yeah.

> (*She climbs off desk, straightens out her hair while He is speaking.*)

HE: (*Continued.*) You just walk in there and give the best presentation that company ever saw!

SHE: They won't know what hit them!

HE: I thought I'd bake some cakes today with the kids. We can have one tonight and freeze the rest for the holidays.

SHE: That sounds great! I'll call you right after the presentation.

HE: Don't worry, honey — you'll be great.

SHE: (*Crossing to door.*) Oh, yeah!! See you tonight.

HE: Dinner will be ready about six, so call if you're going to be late.

SHE: Will do.

HE: Careful — it's a jungle out there.

> (*She howls like a wolf — picks up report — blows him a kiss — leaves.*)

END OF PLAY

CHARACTERS
MONA, twenties
MAN, twenties

TIME
Saturday morning, May 2006

PLACE
The Man's bedroom

• • •

MONA: I don't want to leave.

MAN: Mona—

MONA: I don't ever want to leave this bed. It feels nice.
(After a bit.)

MAN: You should probably think about getting dressed. And I should make up the bed.

MONA: But what if I don't want to go?

MAN: Mona—

MONA: I like it here. I like this room. The walls are a nice color. Soothing.

MAN: Mona—

MONA: That's not my real name, you know—
(When he doesn't respond.)

MONA: *(Continued.)* Don't you want to know my real name?

MAN: What's your real name?

MONA: Sheryl.

MAN: Sheryl?

MONA: Sheryl.

MAN: That's a long way from Mona.

MONA: I like Mona.

MAN: I like Sheryl.
(After a beat.)

MONA: These are nice sheets. What's the thread count? Like a million or something?

MAN: I don't know.

MONA: *(Points to a photograph.)* Is that her?

MAN: *(After a hesitation.)* Yes.

MONA: She's pretty.
(Man shrugs.)

MONA: You don't think she's pretty?

MAN: I think she's pretty.

MONA: Do you love her?

MAN: I love her.

MONA: But you're with me. And you're getting married . . . when? Tomorrow?

MAN: No.

MONA: When?

MAN: Next weekend.

MONA: Oh.

> *(Long silence.)*

MAN: What's going on here?

MONA: What do you mean?

MAN: I mean, why did you come here?

MONA: They paid me to.

MAN: Exactly.

MONA: So.

MAN: This is what you do. It was a bachelor party, right? And my friends hired you because they thought it would be, I don't know, tradition?, and isn't this what you do?

> *(After a silence.)*

You're telling me you've never done this before as part of your . . . service. I mean —

MONA: I know what you mean.

MAN: What —

MONA: You're judging me.

MAN: You're judging me. Do you judge all of your clients like this —

MONA: No.

MAN: Is this some sort of service you perform after the fact, where you try to make the person feel guilty about it, about something no one is ever going to know about? Something that stays right here?

MONA: Now that's the truth.

> *(Beat)*

It does stay here.

MAN: I didn't mean —

MONA: What we did, it stays right here.

MAN: OK.

MONA: It's here.

MAN: I appreciate your . . . discretion. I mean, it's probably part of the package, isn't it?

MONA: Don't tell?

MAN: Exactly. It's sort of like doctor/patient privilege . . . or attorney/client privilege, isn't it? You *are* a professional.

MONA: *(Gets up, walks around, after a bit.)* Have you ever watched a flag?

MAN: What?

MONA: A flag. The way it moves around in the breeze. When the wind catches it just right? The way it wraps itself around the wooden pole, like a dancer?

(She twirls, as if dancing or swinging around a pole.)

MAN: Um, I'm not sure I —

MONA: I didn't think so. Not many people pay that kind of attention.

MAN: What's that supposed to mean?

MONA: *I* pay attention.

(After a moment.)

It's seductive, you know?

MAN: *(Looks at his watch.)* You know you really should be going —

MONA: The American flag is seductive. Like a dancer. It . . . seduces you. I'm not kidding.

And here you are. Living the American dream.

MAN: I'm very lucky. I realize that.

MONA: Nice house. Nice car. . . . Nice girlfriend —

MAN: Fiancée —

MONA: And I'm a woman of mass destruction.

(Beat.)

You're gonna wake up one night with her lying next to you, maybe a kid or two down the hall, maybe they're having a bad night, an ear infection or something, or they're throwing up, whatever, but they're keeping you awake, and you're gonna be lying here cursing your life and wishing you could just go to sleep and make it all go away, make it all disappear, and then it's gonna seep in.

MAN: What?

MONA: It's gonna come out of the walls and enter your head like smoke, or like a dream, and you're gonna be hearing it like a song that won't get the hell out of your head — and you're gonna think of me.

MAN: Please leave.

MONA: And you're gonna wish like hell you never started what you thought was gonna be a good thing, you're gonna wish like hell you could just . . . withdraw . . . and I mean that in *every* sense of the word.

MAN: I won't feel that —

MONA: But it will be too late. And there you'll have it. A quagmire of the heart.

MAN: GET OUT!

MONA: Withdraw?

MAN: Leave. Now.

MONA: Pottery Barn rules. You broke it.

MAN: Get out, please.

MONA: You own it.

END OF PLAY

ARMS

BEKAH BRUNSTETTER

Arms was originally produced as an evening of One Acts at the
New School for Drama, Cohort XI. This production featured
Jane Coutrney and Colin Fischer, and it was directed by
Layne Rackowsky.

CHARACTERS

SIS, twenty

SAM, twenty

Siamese twins, one month after they have been surgically removed from each other. Sis has no left arm. Sam has no right arm.

SETTING

A park bench. Late at night, October, near Halloween. Deserted. A full moon. Crickets. A chill. Somewhere South, i.e., the park is probably sandwiched between a horse farm and a gas station; perhaps a Biscuitville. Quiet.

. . .

Late night, a Park. Sis, twenty, sits on a bench, playing with a bracelet. She is dressed as Mrs. Claus, badly. She has one arm. From somewhere in the dark, a voice, her brother, Sam.

SAM: *(Offstage.)* Sis? Sis, where you at?

SIS: *(Leaping to her feet, waving.)* Over here! I'm by the jungle gym!
(Sam, twenty, enters. He, too, is missing an arm. He is dressed in Marine camos. He is rushed, freaked out, out of breath.)

SAM: Where's the fire?

SIS: What fire?

SAM: You sounded real bad on the phone. What's wrong?

SIS: *(Holding out her bracelet.)* My bracelet fell off and I can't get it back on.

SAM: Seriously?

SIS: What? I can't get it back on. I need you to do it.

SAM: I'm meeting you in the park at two AM cause your bracelet fell off?

SIS: I feel funny without it. Can you just help me get it back on?

SAM: Fine.
(He goes to her. Takes her hand. Helps her put it back on. It may involve teeth. They've done it thousands of times before. It takes a minute.)

SIS: Happy Halloween.

I like your costume.

Camos are cool right now, right? Well that's kind of weird. Kind of ironic, don't you think so? People in the grocery or going to parties dressed like they're ready to shoot somebody. But no, I like it. Looks good. You look like a soldier.
(Pause.)

You going to a party or something? What kinda party? I guess a costume party. I guess that would make sense. I heard Mindy today talking about some party up on Hathaway. She said last year it got busted but by that time, everyone was naked and covered in pumpkin pulp. She said last year, people were doing cocaine. You going to that party? Who drove you here, huh? I don't like you riding around with people. Mom doesn't like it either. She's probably up worrying about us right now. Well not me. Mom thinks I'm in bed. She thinks I went to Mindy's to watch *Dr. Zhivago*. And she said Sis, why are you putting on a costume just to go over to Mindy's and watch a movie, and I said *Mom*.

(Sam is finally done with the bracelet. He looks at her.)

You haven't said you like my costume yet.

SAM: You're Mrs. Claus every year.

SIS: Mom spent a month making it, I have to wear it at least seven times or she'll be sad. Dad says he likes it when I wear it cause it reminds him Christmas is coming. I don't know, it makes me want to bake pies and knit and hug fat people. So, um, what are you doing? Wanna go home and watch Food Network? Secret Life of Potato Chips?

SAM: I don't live there anymore.

SIS: That doesn't mean you can't *visit*.

SAM: Sis.

SIS: Sam?

SAM: We're not supposed to be doing this.

SIS: Doing what?

SAM: We're supposed to be apart. We're supposed to be starting our own lives and learning to live by ourselves. As two different people, separate people. That means not together.

SIS: Who drove you?

SAM: Cass.

SIS: Cass?

SAM: Cass. She works at Baskin Robbins. You haven't met her.

SIS: What's her costume?

SAM: She's some kind of bunny.

SIS: I bet she's not wearing a lot. Slut. *(Pause.)*

SAM: It hasn't even been that long. *(Pause.)* If we keep meeting up like this because you can't find your hair thing or because you want to know what I want for my birthday, we're never going to get anywhere. You're not even *trying*. OK?

SIS: Your shoe's untied. Come here.

SAM: No.

SIS: Sammy, let me do it. Don't be stupid.

SAM: Don't call me stupid.

(She pats the bench next to her. Reluctantly, he sits next to her. They become one. They tie his shoe. They've done it a thousand times. During:)

SIS: Hey remember, I almost forgot, remember when we were eight or something like that, and we would play in the creek down there? And remember Mom said never go near the still water because that's were the bacteria was. And then remember, ha. Remember, there was that one time, right over there, we figured out the monkey bars, how we could do it together. We practiced forever like the Olympics and we did it, and everyone watched. And no one laughed. And then we got popsicles.

SAM: I remember.

SIS: And then remember, the fireworks by the baseball field, and we chased them. Every year.

SAM: Yeah, we did.

SIS: I forget how to run.

SAM: You just have to learn again. To do it by yourself.

SIS: But I don't have anyone to talk to.

SAM: Hey, you said you had a date tonight. With Tommy, from the photo center. He seems really nice.

SIS: I don't know.

SAM: Mindy said you said you gave him a blow job.

SIS: I don't know how to do that.

SAM: And that's *my* problem?!

SIS: Why are you yelling at me?

SAM: I'm not yelling at you!

SIS: I love you.

SAM: I love you too.

(She grabs him, embraces him. He responds. It's tender.)

SIS: What'd you have for dinner?

SAM: Wendy's.

SIS: ME TOO.

(They smile.)

SIS/SAM: Jr.BaconCheeseburgerNoMayoPleaseBiggieFriesBiggieCokeSide BarbequeSauce.

SIS: Was it good?

SAM: Yeah.

SIS: It's like I was there.

SAM: Sort of.

SIS: So exactly. Why are we apart?

SAM: It's not good for us. It was hard enough to get away from each other. It took forever, it was so hard, and now you wanna put it right back.

SIS: But maybe we were wrong for trying. Maybe we could get back together? The thing is. The thing is. I don't know if I like it. I don't like it anymore, being separated from you. I'm not used to it, and it scares me. A lot. I don't like being alone.

SAM: You just gotta try. You're not trying.

SIS: I was eating strawberries the other day. Big fat ones.

SAM: I don't like strawberries.

SIS: **Since when?**

SAM: I just realized it last week that I only ate them a lot because you did.

SIS: Don't say that. You love them. Say you love them.

SAM: Just what about them?

SIS: I was eating them, and I found two stuck together, like freak fruit. Two stuck together like us, cause that happens, when stuff is growing, in nature. Things just join together because it's meant to be. And I cried. And I cried more because I was crying. And I couldn't wipe it on your shirt.

SAM: Wipe it on yourself. *(The car honks.)*

SIS: I don't like her. She's impatient. Doesn't she know you're here with me?

SAM: We have somewhere to be. Plans.

SIS: That don't involve me.

SAM: You could have plans, too.

SIS: I don't want to. And I don't like you riding around with girls dressed like bunnies and going to cocaine parties. Come home with me.

SAM: I don't live there anymore. I go to college. I left. You could, too.

SIS: You go to *community* college, Sam.

SAM: The teachers are really good! They like me! They think I'm smart!

SIS: They feel *sorry* for you!

(Sam starts to go.)

Sam? Sam? I give up. I tried really hard to live not next to you. I told myself over and over how stupid it was to need somebody so bad. I took pictures of us and spit on them. I looked at other people, really looked at them, and tried to see how they were still good, even though they weren't you. I accentuated the positive. Like you said. I didn't call you. Sometimes I don't call you. Even when I want to. I make myself not do it. But I don't feel like it anymore. I give up. Maybe I am insane and maybe I just want to control you and be controlled like you said, or whatever you said, did you say that? But I don't care. I just wanna be back.

Sam? OK. You're ignoring me. That's never happened before. This is the first time anyone has ever ignored anybody at all. Don't you miss me? Even a little bit?

SAM: Of course I miss you.

SIS: When the most?

SAM: At night.

SIS: Me too. *(Pause.)* Come home?

SAM: I can't.

SIS: Why? Because of that girl? What, do you love her or something?

SAM: It's not about her. It's just that, um, I'm kind of leaving. *(Pause.)* See I kind of joined the army. I kind of did that yesterday.
(Long, Long pause.)

SIS: But you only have one arm.

SAM: I'm going to do computer stuff in the government. They just need my brain. They think I'm smart. They want my intelligence. They say I'm an army of one!

SIS: But we don't believe in war.

SAM: No, Sis, *you* don't believe in war! And you never gave me one second to figure out whether or not *I* do! I want to have preferences and I can't do that with you telling what I like all the time! *(Pause.)* So I'm going.

SIS: I hate you. I wish you were never born. I wish you had turned into a period!

SAM: What?

SIS: Why are you leaving? Do you hate me? It's cause I'm a freak, isn't it? Well guess what. SO ARE YOU.

SAM: No, it's cause I love you! Sis! I don't wanna be dead! Do you wanna die?

SIS: *(Quietly)* No.

SAM: If I slept one more night next to you or had to watch you pee one more time or listened to you pop every bone in your hand, I woulda killed you, I swear to God. It woulda been violent. And I love you, but if I have to help you one more time reach the peanut butter or listen to you explain to me what the comics mean, I will murder myself. If I have to listen to you one more time tell someone how much we love strawberries, I will disappear. I want to be somebody. A me. A one thing. By myself. I love you but you eat me. It's better this way. I'm leaving.

SIS: . . . War is evil!

SAM: War is essential.

SIS: You got that outta the newspaper!

SAM: Your costume is stupid!
(Long pause. Sis cries.)
But it is. Christmas-themed Halloween costumes are just stupid.

SIS: Everywhere I go, everywhere I look, I keep thinking everybody has one arm. I stare at them walking to me and I think, look at that. And then it turns out they have two. It was just the way I was looking at them. Or the way they were walking. But it's always just me. And you. I can't sleep anymore. I haven't been sleeping. Do you care?

SAM: You have to learn to.

(A car horn blows in the distance)

Cass's waiting.

SIS: *(Dead.)* What's she like?

SAM: She's quiet. She can tie her own shoe.

SIS: If you go you'll miss my birthday.

SAM: I know I'll miss your fucking birthday. It's mine, too.

SIS: I'm going to be twenty-one. I'm going to get drunk and die.

SAM: Cass and I gotta go. Go home, OK?

SIS: No.

SAM: Go home, and I'll see you.

SIS: When?

SAM: Sometime.

SIS: When?

SAM: Go home.

(Sis grabs Sam again. He pushes her off.)

GO HOME.

(Sam looks at her, lingering, then exits, runs off into the black.)

SIS: . . . OK.

(Her bracelet falls off. She holds it up, and looks out, sniffs.)

SAM! SAM! My bracelet fell off! My bracelet fell off! I FORGET HOW TO DO IT!

SAM!

(Sound of car speeding off. Sis collapses, center, holding her wrist. She's quite a mess. She holds her bare side nostalgically. Slowly, Sam re-enters, she can't see him, but he looks at her, longingly. Almost says something, but turns again, and leaves.)

END OF PLAY

CRIMES AGAINST HUMANITY

ROSS MAXWELL

In Memory of Frank Pisco

CHARACTERS

> FLORA, twenty-four, a brusque young cosmopolitan worker at the United Nations; a long way removed from her Brooklyn background
>
> MICHAEL, nineteen, her brother; much more "street" than his upwardly mobile sister; sarcastic but lovable

TIME AND PLACE

> A cramped and cluttered off-site office of the Human Rights Council at the United Nations. A hot summer night in New York City.

• • •

Lights up on: A small messy office. Flora, twenty-four, has been busy going through drawers and packing a duffel bag. There are stacks of paperwork on a desk. She's dressed very young cosmopolitan business woman. Michael, nineteen, her brother, stands in the doorway with a backpack slung over his shoulder. He's dressed much more "street," and looks out of place in her office space.

FLORA: You really shouldn't be here.

MICHAEL: Uh . . . you're right, it was really nice of me to come all the way into the City to bring you back your stuff. You're welcome.

FLORA: You have five minutes, Michael, and then you gotta go. I'm serious. This is me talking seriously —

MICHAEL: This is you talking seriously.

FLORA: Five minutes.

MICHAEL: Uh-huh.

FLORA: And I didn't ask you to come all the way into the City.

MICHAEL: No, Mom had the wood spoon out, pointing it in my face and telling me I had to come into the City and give you back your shit because she raised such a fucking gentleman. Whaddaya-gonna-do?

(He holds out the backpack. She looks at it, sighs, and grabs it.)

MICHAEL: *(Continued.)* You think I don't have better ways to spend my time?

FLORA: You really want me to answer that?

(Flora looks in the backpack.)

FLORA: *(Continued.)* Oh God, I left this stuff at Mom's on purpose.

MICHAEL: Why would you leave a bag full of your old diaries at Mom's?

FLORA: I bet you read them on the subway ride here.

MICHAEL: No, I didn't read your *diaries* on the way here.

(Beat)

I read that shit years ago.

FLORA: I need you to take them back to Mom's.

MICHAEL: What?! I'm not just taking 'em back there after coming all the way in from Brooklyn. At night. In the heat. Plus, Moms'll still be standing at the front door with that big ass wood spoon in her hand. I'm not giving her any excuses.

FLORA: Fine. Look, whatever. Just leave it here then, I guess. They'll make something of it.

MICHAEL: Who'll make something outta what?

(She turns and stands in front of the desk with her duffel bag on it.)

FLORA: Well, look, thanks for—

(Beat.)

— you know —

(Beat.)

Anyway.

MICHAEL: Anyway.

(Beat. She looks at him. He leans a little to look past her.)

FLORA: You can probably go now, Michael.

(He looks around the small office.)

MICHAEL: So this is the UN, huh? Looks bigger on TV—

FLORA: This is not the UN.

MICHAEL: But I thought you were such a big deal UN intern—

FLORA: *(Overlapping.)* —I never said I was a *big deal*— This is an office of the Human Rights Council of the United Nations. Happy? All clear?

MICHAEL: You work this late because they give you a lot of work?

FLORA: No. I work late because I have initiative.

MICHAEL: What's that mean?

FLORA: It means I don't spend my time chillin' with my boys on Flatbush looking for kids to sell cheap weed to.

MICHAEL: *(As if to a hidden mic.)* I don't know what you're talking about, Flora. I don't use or associate myself with any illegal drugs and/or drug-related substances of any kind.

FLORA: The room's not bugged, you idiot.

MICHAEL: Oh, so you're just being nasty for my benefit. You know, you're starting to sound like they say you sound.

FLORA: Who's "they"?

MICHAEL: Girls back in the neighborhood— saying how you don't call none of them anymore. How you think you're so big and special now.

FLORA: You know what you can tell them when they say that? I am big and special now. I'm up here working on big and special things. I'm not back in Brooklyn, sitting on the stoop, braiding my hair, dressing like a twelve-year-old hooker, waiting for somebody to knock me up.

MICHAEL: I will tell them that.

FLORA: Go ahead.

MICHAEL: I will.

FLORA: Do it.

MICHAEL: Only — you know — I'll make it sound nicer cuz some of those girls are fine.

FLORA: Look, we already hung out at Mom's tonight . . . so, I mean, thanks and all, but I need you to leave now.

MICHAEL: So what big and special stuff you working on that you're in such a hurry?

FLORA: Michael —

MICHAEL: What, is it top secret or something?

FLORA: You actually want to know, or is this just some setup to knock me down?

MICHAEL: I asked, didn't I? Why you being so nasty?

FLORA: I work with a human rights commission to help bring awareness about stopping enforced disappearances. That's when people—

MICHAEL: — are forced to disappear? Yeah, I think I get that. Well, gee, Flora, that sounds . . . really pretty *boring* —

FLORA: *(Simultaneous.)* — *boring*, yeah. I figured. Well, these are crimes against humanity. In South America mostly. People being abducted, erased.

MICHAEL: Forget South America. You got people getting disappeared out in Brooklyn. You remember my buddy Tink?
(Michael starts flipping through some of the things on her desk. As she's talking, he gets to the duffel bag.)

FLORA: Yeah, except I'm talking about people that aren't asking for it. Political dissidents, artists, women. But since nobody really cares about them, it's hard to get any press attention.

MICHAEL: What's in this bag?

FLORA: Nothing's in that bag —

MICHAEL: What, is this, like, your gym bag or something? You working out now — ?

FLORA: Michael, stop messing things up —

MICHAEL: This looks like that time you tried to run away from home when you were a kid.

FLORA: Stop going through my stuff. I'm being serious —

MICHAEL: Hey, what's this —
(Michael pulls out a passport.)

MICHAEL: *(Continued.)* When'd you get a passport?

(Pause. She looks at him. Things click.)

MICHAEL: *(Continued.)* What are you doing?

FLORA: What do you mean, what am I doing? I'm not doing anything. I standing here wondering why you think you have the right to interrogate me.

MICHAEL: You're here in the city late, packing a bag. You want me to take these old *diaries* of yours back to Mom's where you purposely left them tonight . . . You going away someplace I don't know about?
(Pause.)

FLORA: You wouldn't understand —

MICHAEL: Cuz I'm just so stupid and you're so big and special.

FLORA: I'm making a political statement, Michael, and I know that's not your thing, so . . .

MICHAEL: What.

FLORA: Politics. Having a bigger picture. Understanding or caring about what's going on outside your five-block radius.

MICHAEL: It must be pretty hard for you to have such a trashy, narrow-minded, loser brother.

FLORA: Sometimes, yeah.

MICHAEL: And how is running away — ?

FLORA: I'm not running away. I'm disappearing.

MICHAEL: You're doing what?
(She starts to repack the clothes into the duffel bag. She considers.)

FLORA: I'm kidnapping myself. These days, media coverage is all that matters, so I'm going to disappear under mysterious circumstances and that's going to shed light on the issue for the human rights council.

MICHAEL: That is the STUPIDEST thing I ever heard!

FLORA: I'm leaving behind some "clues" here in the office, then I walk out the front door, making sure to say good night to the security guard on-camera. I walk a couple blocks down, turn a corner, and disappear. I'm supposed to meet my friend Nina at a bar in an hour, so when I don't show up, she'll start to get worried. And . . . it'll go from there.

MICHAEL: That's your big and special work? What are you, fuckin' retarded?

FLORA: I knew you wouldn't understand.

MICHAEL: Oh, no, I get it. But it's sick and stupid. And, and what — you just never show up again?
(She shakes her head.)

MICHAEL: *(Continued.)* What about your old friends and your family? What about them?

FLORA: Oh, Michael . . .
(She comes over and hugs him. She pulls back.)

FLORA: *(Continued.) (Hardened.)* What about them.

MICHAEL: So, what — if I didn't come here, tonight at Mom's woulda been the last time?

FLORA: I thought dinner with Mom was a good last time to have — until she got drunk and started yelling —

MICHAEL: She wasn't *drunk. Jesus,* you're such a fuckin' snob —

FLORA: But now we got a problem. You're on-camera coming into the building, so if you don't want to be a part of this, then you need to go now and be on-camera leaving before me.

MICHAEL: I'll tell on you.

FLORA: No, you won't.

MICHAEL: Why not?

FLORA: Because you love me, and because if you ruin this for me, you'll never ever see me again. I'll find other ways to vanish. I won't ever come back to the neighborhood again.

MICHAEL: You don't ever come back now! The girls are right, you really do think you're better than us, don't you?

FLORA: In some ways. No, look, I don't think that, but I don't belong there. Maybe you do, maybe you like that, but I gotta make a bigger world for myself. This is how I'm gonna do it.

MICHAEL: What happens when they don't find you?

FLORA: When the media attention dies down, I can always turn back up eventually and maybe by then, who cares?

MICHAEL: And this is really gonna help your UN cause? Just cuz some pretty girl went missing?

FLORA: Did you just call me pretty?

MICHAEL: — just cuz some dog-faced girl went missing? I'm serious, Flora. I'm talking serious here. Don't do this. Why you always gotta make some big noise of things? Fine, you're a big city deal and I don't know outside my five blocks, but you know what? I know enough not to throw away the people I love.

(Pause. She looks at him.)

MICHAEL: *(Continued.)* Oh. *(Beat.)* I got it. I gotcha.

FLORA: I didn't say that, Michael, but I gotta make a clean break of this —

MICHAEL: A clean break? I get it. You think I'm too dumb to see what you're really about? You're not disappearing because of South America. You're disappearing because of you.

FLORA: I'm disappearing because of you! And Mom. And my whole, *everything.* I finally figured it out. I gotta amputate everything off completely and start over someplace totally new. It's just the only way to survive. You know what I mean?

MICHAEL: No. *(Beat.)* I don't get how you survive without the neighborhood and the people you grew up with. See, that's what I figured out. Why am I out with my boys up and down Flatbush? Cuz I like Flatbush. Fuck the world beyond it! It is the world!

FLORA: It's not mine.

(She picks up the duffel bag.)

FLORA: *(Continued.)* I gotta go, Michael. Five minutes, remember? Which means you gotta go first.

MICHAEL: I can't talk you out of it, can I?

FLORA: I'm already gone.

(He picks up the backpack with the diaries and puts it over his shoulder.)

MICHAEL: On second thought, you know, I think I am gonna haul this shit back out to Brooklyn. You know, cuz, for Mom.

FLORA: Yeah.

MICHAEL: Well, I guess, good luck then . . . liberating South America, or, you know, freeing the people from deception or whatever cloak-and-dagger bullshit you're clinging onto.

FLORA: That's very inspiring, thank you.

MICHAEL: Well, you know, some of us aren't gifted with language. Some of us got other qualities that make us worthwhile.

(As she speaks, Flora picks up a few last things, makes some busy work that takes her eyes away from Michael.)

FLORA: I really wish I could explain this to you, but I don't think you can understand it. And I don't mean that like you're not smart enough to understand it. You're a smart guy, Michael. You and Mom are gonna be fine. What I mean is if you could only experience what this is going to be like from my perspective, maybe you'd see that it's not such a bad thing after all —

(She looks up. Michael's gone. Pause.)

FLORA: *(Continued.)* Maybe you'd see it like I do. *(Beat.)* It's a human rights issue.

(She stands with the duffel bag on her shoulder. She looks at her watch. Beat. She looks at the door. Beat. She looks at her watch. Beat.)

(Lights out.)

END OF PLAY

EVERYTHING IN BETWEEN

SHANNON MURDOCH

Everything in Between was first produced by GB Productions at the North Park Play Festival, North Park Vaudeville and Candy Shoppe, San Diego, California, on 20 October 2006. Director: Gilbert Songalia; Assistant Director: Alma Balderas. Cast: Layla — Michelle D'Alessandro; Franklin — Charles Lawrence Close.

CHARACTERS

LAYLA, thirty-two years old. Caught the travel bug late in life and now can't seem to stand still for very long. She is happy to be constantly on the move, searching for the unnameable something that is missing from her life.

FRANKLIN, thirty-two years of age. Impatient and quick to lose his temper when things don't run to his schedule. Subsequently, Franklin constantly finds himself out of his depth in situations and acting appropriately.

STAGING

The stage is divided down the center with a white line, into Franklin and Layla's space. During the play, neither enters into the other's space. Franklin's space has one chair. Layla's is bare. The sparseness of the stage enables the characters to move through different places seamlessly.

TIME

Present

• • •

Lights up on Layla's space. She is standing at the end of an invisible queue, waiting. She pops her head out to the side and stands on her toes, trying to see why the queue is not moving. She is impatient, bored, frustrated, and tired. She has a large backpack on her back and wears loose, comfortable clothing. A moment passes.
Layla sighs dramatically.
She turns, sharply and her backpack knocks the person in front of her (imagined) to the ground.

LAYLA: Oh shit. Sorry.
  (Layla bends down as far as she can go, with an enormous backpack on her shoulders and extends an arm to help the person up.)
LAYLA: Are you alright?
  You sure?
  (Beat.)
  Do you know what's going on here?
  I hate this. It always happens. This waiting.
  This waiting and waiting and waiting. It's horrible. Nothing but a slow tumbling towards madness.

(Lights up on Franklin in his space. He sits on a chair, facing the white line. He has a bunch of flowers that are beginning to wilt.)

(He waits impatiently. His leg bounces up and down and his head is darting side to side so much he looks like he has a severe twitch.)

(When he can't bear it any longer, he jumps up out of his chair and starts pacing. At the same time, Layla begins tapping her foot in rhythm with Franklin's movements.)

FRANKLIN: *(To another person that is sitting beside him.)* Do you know what's happened? Has something happened? Because, the screen . . . the TV screen . . .

LAYLA: *(To the woman in front of her.)* It's just that —

FRANKLIN: The TV screen says that it has landed.

The plane has landed.

LAYLA: I wouldn't normally mind. I've been doing this a while now. A long while . . . and I understand. Things don't run smoothly. Delays can be experienced.

But today . . . Today I'm on a pretty tight schedule today.

Really tight.

FRANKLIN: The plane landed over an hour ago. Well over an hour ago.

LAYLA: Shit. I mean, damn. Damn.

FRANKLIN: I know these things take time.

LAYLA: Damn it all to hell.

FRANKLIN: I'm not what you would call a world traveller . . . but I'm not a fucking idiot either.

These things take time.

LAYLA: Deep breaths Layla. Sometimes there are delays. Sometimes things don't run to my plan. I get that.

FRANKLIN: It takes time to get from the plane to here.

LAYLA: It's just that this is really important.

FRANKLIN: But this much? Should it take this much time?

LAYLA: I can't fuck this up.

FRANKLIN: Are you waiting for this plane? No?

Well, that's just great.

LAYLA: I mean, well . . . I mean I can't fuck this up. That's exactly what I mean.

FRANKLIN: I've waited.

LAYLA: This is my last chance.

FRANKLIN: I'm here and I waited.

LAYLA: I'm at the end of my line. I can feel the rope running out.

FRANKLIN: You can't take that from me.

LAYLA: And then what?

FRANKLIN: I'm here. And I waited.

LAYLA: What comes at the end of the rope?

FRANKLIN: There's no way she can ask for more than that.

> *(A moment passes.)*
>
> *(Franklin goes and dumps the wilted flowers in the bin.)*
>
> *(The bin is of course not there, and he does it with such force that they scatter all over the stage, both on Franklin's side and on Layla's.)*
>
> *(The tension breaks.)*
>
> *(Everything slows down.)*
>
> *(Franklin and Layla begin moving around their respective spaces. Slow, wandering circles that have little shape or structure.)*
>
> *(During the next set of vignettes, they stop together, play the scene and then continuing moving. Every time they stop, it is a new time and place.)*

First Stop

> *(Franklin stops suddenly. Then Layla does the same thing. Franklin seems out of breath, tired, defeated. He collapses into the chair.)*

FRANKLIN: I don't know if you'll get this. I don't know if you are getting any of these messages.

LAYLA: I got your message. It was this huge hassle but . . . well, it doesn't matter.

But it was funny. It was really funny.

> *(Franklin begins to heave, trying not to cry.)*

FRANKLIN: Well, I don't know.

I don't know how I'm supposed to know if you're hearing any of this.

LAYLA: It took me forever to find somewhere to get my messages. That's what you get for going off the beaten track I guess.

FRANKLIN: You tell me that Layla.

You come home and tell me how on earth I am supposed to know what is going on?

> *(They continue walking. Layla stops then Franklin stops.)*

LAYLA: I'm here. I'm finally here. You should see it Franklin.

Africa rocks.

FRANKLIN: Jesus. Jesus, I didn't want to do this.

LAYLA: I wish you were here.

FRANKLIN: The fucking cat died.

LAYLA: This is the best thing ever!

FRANKLIN: I don't know. I don't know what happened.

She just fucking died. Fuck.

LAYLA: But you're not here. You're there. So . . .

FRANKLIN: It wasn't my fault. For once, I did everything right.

LAYLA: Anyway, I've got to go. I'm going to miss my plane. I'm flying into the jungle tonight.

(They begin walking again. They both stop at the same time. Layla is crying.)

FRANKLIN: Great news! I got that promotion.

LAYLA: What do you mean she died? How can a cat just die? Just like that? What does that mean Franklin?

FRANKLIN: I'm going out to celebrate.

LAYLA: I'm coming home.

(A moment passes.)

(Both start walking again.)

SECOND STOP

(Layla stops near the audience, facing them. Franklin stops wherever he is, facing the audience also. Layla pulls out a large wad of cash from her pocket and thrusts it toward the audience.)

LAYLA: Here . . . This is all the money I have. Every last cent of it. Now . . . can you help me? Can you get me out of here?

(Layla holds the pose for a moment, and then she stuffs the money back into her pocket. During this last vignette, Franklin and Layla mirror facial expressions. Upbeat, expectant.)

(Hold.)

(Deflated, defeated. They begin walking again.)

THIRD STOP

(Layla stops and pulls out a pen.)

(Franklin stops, facing away from the audience. Layla begins writing in the air.)

LAYLA: Dear Franklin,

You just got to hold on for two weeks. Two weeks. That's it. And then I'll be home.

For a while.

I tried to come home for the cat, for Isobel . . . But jungle people don't understand the significance of dead cats.

I'm in Mexico. Near the beach, learning how to fly . . . kites. We make them and then we fly them. And then we sell them to the tourists.

I don't expect you to understand. I know this doesn't . . . I know I don't fit in with your plans, any of them.

But this is where I need to be. I need to fly kites. I need to run along beaches and make my kites fly high into the heavens.

I don't expect you to understand.

(Beat.)

Just hold on Franklin. Just hold on.

Love Layla.

(Layla stops, pen still poised in the air. She holds that pose for a moment. Both start walking.)

Fourth Stop

(Franklin stops suddenly at the front of the audience. Layla stops in the same position she was at the beginning. Waiting in the queue.)

FRANKLIN: You don't understand.

Waiting. All this waiting. You don't know what that does to a man.

And I know. I know that I deserve every last second of it. I know that I could never wait long enough or well enough . . . to make everything alright again.

(Beat.)

I know that I love her. I know that much.

I know that means that I should be able to wait forever. Stand alone, comforted by my love for her, and just wait it out.

But, come on. For the love of God . . . Really. Come on.

(Beat.)

And I know.

I'm acting like a crazy man. You want to call security or run away. You want to wrestle me to the ground, make me stop.

(Beat.)

I just need her to walk through those doors.

I need that.

LAYLA: *(To the woman in front of her in the queue.)* You see, there's a man on the other side of that door.

A man that loves me but is getting very sick of waiting for me to forgive him.

FRANKLIN: I'm sick.

I'm sick and tired of being alone. Of waiting. Of not knowing if it's going to work out in the end . . . or if it's just going to end.

LAYLA: He thinks what I'm doing, what I have done, is punishment.

And don't get me wrong. For a long time, I wanted him punished. Payback or retribution or something. Something to make the hurt worthwhile. To give it meaning.

(Beat.)

But it doesn't work out like that.

FRANKLIN: Yes.

Yes, you know what happened. I can see the look on your face. I can see that you know that I cheated on her.

(Beat.)

That I freaked out. That I tried to push the limits. Tried to see what I could get away with. Tried to be bigger and more powerful than is possible for a man like me to ever be.

(Beat.)

I was a stupid fucking prick OK?

And I know that you know that.

So please . . . please, can you tell me if the people that got off that plane from Mexico that landed nearly two hours ago, have come through Customs yet.

(Beat.)

Good.

Thank you. That's all I needed to know.

(Layla suddenly begins moving quickly up to the front of the stage, still standing in her queue.)

LAYLA: Oh my God. Would you look at that. We're moving. We're actually moving.

(Layla pulls out a form from her pocket and hands it to a security officer.)

LAYLA: Thank you. Thank you so much.

(Layla moves rapidly to the front of the audience and stops. Franklin mimics her actions. They are both facing the audience. They smile. A moment passes.)

LAYLA: Well.

FRANKLIN: Yes.

(Beat.)

You look great. Tired, but great.

LAYLA: You too. Tired, but great.

(Beat.)

FRANKLIN: Layla.

LAYLA: Franklin.

(Beat.)

FRANKLIN: I had flowers.

I brought flowers. For you.

LAYLA: It's OK Franklin.

FRANKLIN: Yeah?

LAYLA: Yeah.

(A moment passes.)

(Blackout.)

END OF PLAY

FALLOUT

S. W. SENEK

Fallout was originally presented in New York City at Polaris North, October 2006 as part of an evening of theater called *The American Woman Project.* This play was directed by Julie Jensen. Cast: Harold — Mickey Ryan; Janet — Joan Lunoe.

CHARACTERS

JANET

HAROLD

TIME

October 1961, one year before the Cuban missile crisis

PLACE

In the basement of a married couple's home — in a homemade fallout shelter. It is a dimly lit space with an abundance of boxes stacked.

• • •

In the September (1961) issue of Life *magazine, President Kennedy advised, in a letter, that Americans build fallout shelters — causing a wave of "shelter mania." This lasted about a year.*

Harold and Janet, in their late thirties/early forties, are in the midst of putting on their protective suits — they look more like cheap yellow rain coats/trousers. Harold wears a stopwatch around his neck.

JANET: I have to get out.

HAROLD: No, we don't have time. Put the suit on. *(He looks at his stopwatch.)* My watch says six minutes, fifteen seconds — that's practically six minutes.

JANET: I know how long six minutes is.

HAROLD: *(Listening to a sound coming from above.)* Wait — did you hear that?

JANET: What?

HAROLD: Shhh — I thought I heard something — upstairs.

JANET: It's the cat. Pickles. Harold, it's hot — I'm suffocating.

HAROLD: No, you're not. Where's my other boot?

JANET: My zipper's broke —

HAROLD: Did you move my boot?

JANET: I said my zipper is — I can't.

HAROLD: You have to. *(He looks at his stopwatch.)* Janet — hurry. *(He puts single boot on.)* Forget the zipper and boot — checklist — checklist! *(Holds up a clipboard.)* Let's get the blankets ready. Survival, Janet, survival.

JANET: I'm tired.

HAROLD: Do you think the Russians care if you're tired? Fourteen minutes — fourteen minutes — that's how fast these bombs are. *(Looking for the labeled box of blankets.)* Where's the blanket box? Why aren't the labels facing out?

JANET: Harold, how many times? We get up in the middle of the night — down here — stay up all night — reload supplies all day — sleep for a half hour — down here — how long do we have to do these drills? *(Harold opens a box and pulls out a shredded blanket.)* It's insane.

HAROLD: Did you let Pickles down here?

JANET: Me?

HAROLD: I told you not to — that's it — the cat's gone! *(Harold pantomimes strangling.)*

JANET: But you like Pickles —

HAROLD: A goner I tell you! Checklist! *(Looks at what's next on the checklist.)* Flashlights.

JANET: How many more nights of these drills? They're going to fire you —

HAROLD: Let them. This is more important — are you sure you didn't hear anything up stairs?

JANET: The dealership called, Harold. You can't stop showing up for work. We need the money — and I want sleep — Pickles wants sleep.

HAROLD: No, you want to live.

JANET: No, I want to sleep.

HAROLD: Stop this. We agreed. *(Searching in a box.)* We should have two more flashlights.

JANET: We're going crazy — that's what we're doing — that's what *I'm* doing.

HAROLD: When that bomb hits, you're going to be thanking me. Now where the hell are the other flashlights? It should be in the box labeled flashlights.

JANET: If a nuclear bomb hits, I'm not thanking anyone.

HAROLD: This is no time for jokes.

JANET: Who's joking? With six minutes left, I'm not joking.

HAROLD: *(Looking at stopwatch.)* Four minutes, forty seconds — Christ you've wasted over a minute. We're running behind schedule. Double check the powdered milk while I look for the flashlights. *(He continues looking through boxes.)*

JANET: Don't you see what this is doing to you?

HAROLD: Time Janet, time. How many powdered milks?

JANET: Twenty-two. That's how many we had last night — how many we had the night before — how many we had when we started. That's how many we bought!

HAROLD: Christ, I don't need your attitude.

JANET: What do you need from me?

HAROLD: Where's the powdered milk? I need you to take this seriously.

JANET: I am — I have been.

HAROLD: Flashlights, Janet! Four minutes, ten seconds! Do you know how behind we are? Do you? *(She sits.)* Wait what are you doing? Sitting? You can't sit. No — get up and help me. If you don't, we'll do it again. Is that what you want?

JANET: No, Harold.

HAROLD: This is serious stuff. I mean Kennedy said — *(Grabs news clipping.)* it's right here! The Russians could attack us. And you know he doesn't joke. We have to be prepared. Kennedy said —

JANET: *(Mockingly.)* "Kennedy said — Kennedy said."

HAROLD: When this thing hits Janet — and it will — it will level everything. The schools, post office, library, your goddamn hair salon — people — family. But not us, you hear me? And all those neighbors —

JANET: The ones that look at us funny —

HAROLD: They look at us funny because they're not prepared — the hell with them. They don't believe. *(Looks at stopwatch.)* Three and a half minutes! Checklist!

JANET: *(Mockingly.)* Three and a half minutes! Three and a half minutes! Checklist!

HAROLD: Don't mock me.

JANET: *(Mockingly.)* "Don't mock me."

HAROLD: And where's the water? Did you refill the water bottles today? Where's the fresh water?

JANET: I forgot.

HAROLD: You what?! What good is the powdered milk without water?

JANET: I forgot — the bottles are in the garage.

HAROLD: Christ, how could you forget — do you know how important it is to have fresh water? Everyday I say refill — and where are the flashlights!

JANET: Everyday — I'm sick of filling up one hundred and fifty-two bottles of water! Earthly sick of it! Do you know that yesterday when I was filling them up in the bath tub, I about drowned? I slipped and hit my head. Did you even ask about the bump on my head? No.

HAROLD: Why is *this* box empty?

JANET: Don't you care? I could have been dead filling up these goddamn bottles up for a bomb that will never hit us! That's right — I don't think it will hit us. I think it's all a crock of — of —

HAROLD: Don't you even finish that thought.

JANET: I'm right.

HAROLD: *We* did this together — together.

JANET: No, *you* did this. I did it for you. All I heard for six weeks was, "a shelter Janet, that's the only way we'll survive." I agreed because that's the only way I could survive with you — if I heard you mention the shelter one more day —

HAROLD: This is a fine time — *(Looks at the stopwatch again.)* Christ — less than two minutes! Now's not the time for this. Unbelievable! This box has bricks in it —

JANET: Unbelievable? You're unbelievable — do you know how much money we've spent on this junk?

HAROLD: Now it's junk?

JANET: Yes! It's junk.

HAROLD: Well, we'll have tons of money after the goddamn bomb hits — tons! All those idiots that didn't protect themselves — it'll be like a free bank when we get out of here.

JANET: Will you listen to yourself? Everyone will be dead! There'll be nothing to buy!

HAROLD: Another box of bricks — who put these in here? Janet? Where are all the cans of food?

JANET: They're in the kitchen — where they belong.

HAROLD: They belong down here! Christ — *(Looks at his stopwatch.)* minute twenty! Now we'll have nothing to eat. How are we supposed to survive without food and water?! And where's my flashlight!!

JANET: We have each other.

HAROLD: You — YOU! You did this? AHHHH!

JANET: I left Band-Aids.

HAROLD: What?

JANET: In case we get cut.

HAROLD: Everything up above is going to be destroyed, and you managed to keep the Band-Aids. *(Looks at his stopwatch.)* Fifty seconds — forget the list — we have to get into position.

JANET: I'm not getting into position.

HAROLD: No, you have to — *(He tries to take her, but she breaks free.)*

JANET: And crouch for what — the next two hours.

HAROLD: That's what we're supposed to do.

JANET: Not me.

HAROLD: Why are you doing this? Survival, Janet — survival!

JANET: I'm not getting into that ridiculous position.

HAROLD: You have thirty seconds, Janet — do you hear me! Thirty seconds before it all blows up!

JANET: Bon Voyage!

HAROLD: Well, I'm getting down! You'll be sorry.

JANET: Then do it.

HAROLD: *(He gets down on the floor.)* Don't make me live like this — now get down! Please!

JANET: No.

HAROLD: Fifteen seconds. Janet! You listen to me goddamn it! Twelve, eleven, ten, nine — Janet — seven, six, five, four, three, two, one! *(Beat of silence.)* JANET!!!!!! GODDAMN IT — YOU'RE DEAD! ARE YOU HAPPY NOW! YOU RUINED IT! YOU SABATOGED ME — THIS — EVERYTHING!

JANET: Good.

HOWARD: Good? GOOD?! CHRIST! What if this was real! YOU'RE GOD-DAMN DEAD. DEAD, DEAD!!

JANET: Don't you get it? I DON'T CARE! *(Beat.)* I can't take living in fear anymore! It's everywhere we go — the television — the radio — news-papers — that's all people talk about — that's all you ever talk about. Don't you see what it's done to us? We used to talk about dinner, children, how many cars you sold — we were normal. Now you're possessed and I don't even know you anymore. Every waking moment it's the shelter — get the food for the shelter, paint the shelter, breakfast, lunch and dinner in the shelter, drills in the shelter — reading in the shelter, boxes in the shelter, blankets, water, powdered milk — our whole life in this God forsaken shelter. Right now, I wish the bomb would hit this shelter and take us from our misery. BOOM! BOOOOOOM!!

HAROLD: Janet, they're out there — Communists — they don't believe like we do — they don't have freedom like we do — they hate us. They're wait-ing to get us. Waiting with their ships in the ocean or God knows where — off the coast — Christ, in our back yard — upstairs even.

JANET: Then so be it — there's nothing we can do.

HAROLD: You're wrong. We have this. Survival, Janet — survival! GODDAMN SURVIVAL!

JANET: I DON'T WANT TO SURVIVE! *(Pause.)* I'm sorry, Harold, but I don't want to be the only ones living. Don't you see, I couldn't bear to walk out of here and not recognize anything because it's been leveled — and say "hey, remember such in such was there — remember so and so — and here's their foot bone." No. I'd be like dying twice — dying alone. I like my memories the way they are — the schools, the children — you stand-ing in the lot trying to sell Cadillacs. I don't want that to change. And I can't keep living like this every single day. This right now — *this* is killing me.

HAROLD: Well, you're wrong. And you know it. Checklist! *(Looks at the checklist.)* Now I have to make a replacement list. First, flashlights. *(Knocks some boxes over in frustration.)* Where did you put the flashlights!

JANET: Harold, let's leave this lunacy.

HAROLD: Now it's lunacy? Well, we got a war to fight — and I'm doing my part . . . with or without you. Now as soon as I restock everything, I'm running the drill again, and again, and again. Until its right. *(Beat.)* Shhhh — did you hear that?

JANET: Hear what — I didn't hear anything.

HAROLD: That — I heard a noise — again. Upstairs. *(He crouches behind some boxes.)*

JANET: It's Pickles.

HAROLD: Christ. They're here. Them — THEM! Spies.

JANET: Harold! Please.

HAROLD: They're up there.

JANET: There's nobody up there! Harold —

HAROLD: Shhh —

JANET: *(She removes her suit.)*
Harold . . . I can't take this anymore. *(Beat.)* I'm going to Mom's or June's.

HAROLD: Don't go — please, they're up there. Get behind the boxes — hurry.

JANET: No. *(Pause.)* I'm going — and I'm taking Pickles with me.

HAROLD: Janet — don't go up. They'll take you. Please Janet — I'm begging you — begging! *(He grabs her.)* We're safe here. We're survivors. We have to survive.

JANET: HAROLD! LET ME GO!!

HAROLD: *(He lets go.)* Alright — alright — shhhh, shhhh. Goddamn it — fine. *(Dives back into the boxes.)* Don't tell them that I'm down here. Promise me.

JANET: *(Finishes removing her suit.)* There's no one up there —

HAROLD: *(He reaches out and grabs her again more sternly.)* Just promise me.

JANET: *(Frustrated.)* Harold — *(Trying to make sense of his state of mind.)* I promise. *(He lets go and stacks the boxes.)* I hope it ends soon. *(Beat.)* Goodbye, Harold.

HAROLD: *(He momentarily stops stacking boxes and looks at Janet. Loud whisper.)* You'll be sorry. Whether they get you upstairs — or when the bomb hits — you'll see — you'll be sorry!
(Beat. He continues stacking the boxes. Janet slowly exits. Blackout.)

END OF PLAY

HEARTBREAKER

Michael Golamco

Heartbreaker was a selected ten-minute play for *Ten*, a special staged reading celebrating the Tenth Anniversary of Second Generation Productions in New York City. April 30th and May 1st, 2007, at the Public Theater, 425 Lafayette Street, New York, N.Y. Cast: Vuthy — Matthew G. Park; Ra: Jackie Chung.

CHARACTERS

VUTHY, male, sixteen

RA, female, twenty-two

SETTING

A small, empty apartment bedroom in Long Beach, California. The present.

. . .

A small, empty bedroom. Vuthy (pronounced "woo-tee"), sixteen, Cambodian American, carries in a duffle bag of his things; he has thick-ass glasses and is so skinny that they probably keep him from blowing away.

He's followed in by his sister Ra, twenty-two, normal. She's got another box of his stuff, puts it down.

RA: So you got all your things . . . And Aunt Tizz is gonna drive you to pick up your computer later.

(He sits, doesn't say anything.)

RA: Hey, look at all this space. Nice . . . Window. Finally some sunlight for you. Lotsa blank walls for whatever you wanna put up on them —

VUTHY: I need my computer now.

RA: She's gonna drive you to pick it up later. I gotta go, traffic on the Five's gonna get crazy if I don't leave right now —

(She hugs him.)

VUTHY: She isn't even our aunt.

RA: You know how much of a big heart she's gotta have to open up her home to you?

VUTHY: She isn't even related to us. She's just a lady that Ma used to play mahjong with —

RA: You gotta start being more grateful. Social services isn't gonna let a sixteen-year-old kid live by himself —

VUTHY: I'm mature for my age.

RA: You still buy toys —

VUTHY: VINTAGE TIN ROBOTS. VINTAGE TIN ROBOTS and they're still in their boxes which makes me a collector of vintage tin robots. I don't *play*, Ra.

RA: Sure.

(Short pause.)

VUTHY: It smells like mothballs and cat pee in here. And I gotta get my computer —

RA: It wouldn't hurt you to stay off that thing for a coupla days, y'know. Lay off the video games.

VUTHY: I don't play video games. I told you: I only do pen-and-paper role playing. It's more visceral. I gotta get it 'cause I wanna see if I got any e-mail from Bert.

RA: The e-mail from Bert can wait. I gotta go.

(She hugs him again.)

VUTHY: Hey I heard they have this real great comic book store in Berkeley —

RA: Vuthy —

VUTHY: That's run by this crazy beardo hippie who's all nazi with the comics, and this place is like a museum of art-Fort-Knox — they got the 1940 All American with the first appearance of The Green Lantern under glass. An if the hippie doesn't like how you look he hits a button and it drops down underneath a blast shield —

RA: It's the middle of the school year.

VUTHY: So what?

RA: It would be bad to move you right now, put you in a brand-new school —

VUTHY: So what.

RA: So you gotta stay here with Aunt Tizz and then we'll see —

VUTHY: I don't care if I move, Ra. I wanna move. They hate me at Lakewood High. You remember how Justin Vu accidentally stabbed me with a pencil?

RA: Yeah.

VUTHY: It wasn't an accident. I'm pretty sure I'm gonna be murdered by senior year.

RA: You've got friends.

VUTHY: Bert moved. See I'm too Cambodian for the black and Latino kids and I'm not Cambodian enough for the Cambodian kids.

RA: What does that mean?

VUTHY: *Look at me,* Ra. And they got the mad dogg stare down — that whatchoo lookin at sucka stare down — but whenever I try to do it my gently arching eyebrows betray me.

RA: My place in Berkeley's just one room and a hot plate. We sleep on a futon, and Glenn's got all his stuff packed in there —

VUTHY: Oh yeah, you're living with the whitest white man from Orange County —

RA: *(Defensively.)* He's not that white —

VUTHY: "Glenn" with two *n*'s? Oh yeah he is. He's so white that I'm still not exactly sure what he looks like 'cause he appears as this huge blinding silhouette —

RA: So you know there's no space what with His Blindingness in there. You gotta stay here, Vuthy. I can't take you.

VUTHY: Ra —

RA: I can't.

(Ra unzips his duffle bag, begins to unpack it.)

RA: Look, you got an even better setup here than you did back in our old place. You got more space, it's closer to the library — OH SHIT —

(She whips her hand away from his bag; he leans over to see —)

VUTHY: What? Oh, that.

RA: What the fuck is that?!

(Vuthy reaches into the bag —)

VUTHY: OK, remember three years ago, I was thirteen and you were a senior and we went on that Khmer group trip to Choeung Ek, and they had that temple in the middle of the field —

RA: Oh my god, Vuthy —

VUTHY: And inside, they had all these racks inside, like right there in front of you. And on them there were hundreds, thousands of them, these —

RA: Please tell me you didn't —

VUTHY: Close enough to touch. One of them just seemed outta place, Ra. It was just a little one, and I coulda sworn I heard it call to me. It was like, *Hey kid* —

RA: Fuck, Vuthy!

VUTHY: *I been here too long, kid. My eyes been seeing the same sad faces . . . They look into me always expectin' to see sorrow back . . . I wanna run. Take me with you — I wanna see this place called Long Beach . . .*

So when no one was looking I —

(He produces a human skull.)

VUTHY: Popped it into my backpack.

RA: Do you know how totally monstrous and insane that is?

VUTHY: No.

RA: VUTHY. That was someone's fucken head. Someone's bodily remains — you had no right —

VUTHY: I take good care of it, Ra.

RA: I don't care! . . . Oh my god!

VUTHY: You gotta care for the dead.

RA: So this is what you do? You steal their skulls?

VUTHY: *(Thinking.)* This is somebody who ran. They ran and got caught. Ma

ran and didn't get caught, and that's how come you and me can go back
and see what they did, see all the people that ran and got caught —

RA: So what.

VUTHY: So when this one said, "Take me with you," I had to take it, Ra. Had
to.

RA: It's a crime.

VUTHY: What?

RA: Importing human remains, bones, over international . . . Whatever — you
gotta bury it, Vuthy. Do something, please.

VUTHY: OK, Ra —

RA: Shit — do you know how many times I prayed to have a normal little
brother? God, Jesus, please give me a normal little brother that I don't
have to worry about. But for some reason you don't know how to be normal —

VUTHY: I'm trying as hard as I can —

RA: You made Ma sick by gettin' picked on all the time, by being weird, by
having no friends. Sick with worry. You broke her heart with worry.

VUTHY: I just wanted to help somebody run away —

RA: For once, OK, put away the heartache, leave the past behind, stop talking
about shit that happened a long time ago. "They ran." So what.
(A pause.)

VUTHY: . . . You didn't want to go. Three years ago, when we went to Cam-
bodia, you didn't want to go.

RA: But I had to go.

VUTHY: At Choeung Ek, you stayed outside the temple.
(Beat.)
You wouldn't go in.

RA: . . . Ma made me go.

VUTHY: You didn't wanna go? You said that you did.

RA: That's the past. That's . . .

VUTHY: You seemed like you did.

RA: Ma didn't want you to go alone. But you of course wanted to go, so I had
to go with you.

VUTHY: You didn't have to.

RA: Yeah I did, Vuthy.

VUTHY: Oh . . . Thanks, Ra.
(Beat.)
Hey, Ra . . .
(Re: the skull)

I didn't steal it from the temple at Choeung Ek. I bought it offa the Internet — museum quality replica, thirty-nine dollars shipped.

(She punches him in the arm twice.)

VUTHY: Ow ow.

RA: I hate you so.

VUTHY: *(Grinning.)* You believed though.

RA: Why the fuck can't you be normal?

VUTHY: I don't know, I don't think about it.

(A beat, then re: the skull.)

Though when I look at this I remember Choeung Ek. I think about Ma running, all by herself with wet feet through the long grass.

(Beat.)

Been thinking about that a lot lately . . . I think about all those skulls on the rack lookin' at me askin' me what I did to deserve Ma's gettin' away.

RA: You think too much.

VUTHY: I got no friends since Bert moved. Got nothing to do but think.

RA: Yeah, well . . . I just wanna be happy, Vuthy. That's all.

VUTHY: Livin' with the whitest white man from Orange County.

RA: *(Laughs.)* He's not that white.

VUTHY: He's polar bear white. Translucent-North-Pole-snowman-style. He got a carrot for a nose.

RA: He makes me laugh. And he hasn't made me cry.

VUTHY: Yet.

RA: Yet.

(Ra suddenly picks up Vuthy's box of things.)

RA: C'mon. Get your stuff. We're going.

VUTHY: Really, Ra? Really really?

RA: Get your stuff before I change my mind.

(Vuthy grabs his duffle bag.)

VUTHY: What about my computer?

RA: We'll swing by, get it right now.

(He hugs her. Her arms are full of his things. She starts to head out —)

RA: But.

VUTHY: But what?

RA: You gotta promise me: Don't turn me into Ma. Do not make me worry. I'm not like she was — I can't take it. Can you promise me that?

VUTHY: Ra . . .

RA: Can you?

VUTHY: You know me. I can't promise anything.

RA: Then . . . I guess we'll just have to see.

(Ra exits.)

(Vuthy regards the skull.)

VUTHY: All right. We shall see this place called Berkeley . . . And believe-you-me, we're gonna test the hell outta this comic book nazi!

(He exits with his duffle bag.)

END OF PLAY

PIE AND THE SKY

Vanessa David

Originally produced July 8 and 9, 2006, by Eastbound Theatre in association with SquareWrights at the Milford Center for the Arts in Milford, Connecticut. Cast: Max — Sam Cocks; Jess — Lisa Westfall. Directed by Suzanne Coughlin. Producer, Tom Rushen.

CHARACTERS

MAX, early to middle thirties

JESS, late twenties early thirties

SETTING

A field, a sky . . . or a bare stage

• • •

MAX: *(Offstage.)* This is it! *(On stage, photo in hand.)* This is it! It's gotta be it! *(Yelling offstage.)* Hun, this is it! This is the place! *(To himself.)* I can't believe I found it from a picture. This is good, it's a sign. *(Yelling offstage again.)* Jess, c'mon! This is it! This is the place. Put that finger away and just come over here sweetie.

(Jess enters. She is wearing what she slept in, wrapped in a blanket.)

MAX: *(Continued.)* Look, baby, this is it! This is the place.

JESS: I'm freezing.

MAX: C'mon, you're always cold, sweetie.

JESS: Where on God's green earth have you taken me, where it's cold in August?

MAX: It's not cold.

JESS: It *is* August . . . unless I slept through the rest of August. Ya never know — I did wake up in a car, in transit to God knows where — I could've been out for a few weeks, I suppose.

MAX: One night only — you drank too much and passed out. I took advantage, I'll admit it, I'm your husband.

JESS: You took advantage of me?

MAX: No, I just put you in the car while you were out.

JESS: And brought me here?

MAX: Yeah.

JESS: Where it's cold in August . . .

MAX: Yeah.

JESS: And where is here? Where it's cold in August . . .

MAX: Does it matter?

JESS: Yeah.

MAX: It's not Fairfield County . . .

JESS: I can see that Max. Where are we, Canada?

MAX: Close, it's a few miles that way.

JESS: A few miles?! How long did you have me in the car?!?

MAX: C'mon, you know how you sleep when you've been drinking.

JESS: I had three drinks!

MAX: In a half hour!

JESS: No — it was, like, 45 minutes. C'mon, I worked ten hours with that woman — let me at least have a drink when I get home.

MAX: I'm not saying you can't have a drink — but three drinks in a half hour/forty-five minutes ain't a road I want my wife traveling down.

JESS: Did you drive me to Sasquatchewan to give me an intervention?

MAX: *(Laughing.)* It's Saskatchewan, it's Native American and it's way, way, that way.

JESS: Whatever, I could do without the geography lesson and your intervention.

MAX: Sweetie —

JESS: And how come you could manage to kidnap me in my sleep and drive me to where ever the hell we are, but you left me in my jammies. *(Max laughs.)* What's so funny?

MAX: How am I supposed to take you seriously when you say jammies.

JESS: C'mon, why couldn't you manage to put a sweater on me . . .

MAX: Here, take mine . . .

JESS: Sweetie, that's not the point . . . .

MAX: Well, you keep saying you're cold, so take the sweater.

JESS: Well then you're gonna be cold.

MAX: No I won't, I'll be fine.

JESS: Are you sure?

MAX: I'm positive, take the sweater.

JESS: Well if you're not gonna be cold, why didn't you give me the sweater before we got out of the car?

MAX: Hun —

JESS: I'm just bustin' on ya, gimme the sweater . . .

MAX: You're a real pain in the ass sometimes . . .

JESS: I love you too . . .

MAX: Better now, dear?

JESS: Once you tell me why we're here, dear . . .

MAX: Here, honey, look at the picture.

JESS: What do I need the picture for, I'm here . . .

MAX: Just look at the picture. I've got coffee and pie in the car.

JESS: You packed coffee and pie and you didn't bring me a sweater.

MAX: You've got a sweater now sweetie . . . look at the picture and tell me what you see . . .

JESS: *(Overlapping.)* Grass, sky . . .

MAX: *(Exiting to car.)* Wait! Tell me over coffee and pie.

JESS: *(To herself.)* Coffee and pie . . . *(Yelling after him.)* That better not be one of her pies!

MAX: *(Offstage.)* It's not! It's a supermarket pie.

JESS: I'm the only person who works at a bakery and refuses to eat the food. *(Looking at photo.)* That's amazing, the trees are spaced right. Boy, when my husband sets his mind to something . . . What is he, insane? There's nothing for miles. *(Beat.)* Maybe I could get used to this. *(Referring to photo.)* Makes it look like this is the —

MAX: *(Entering with a cooler and cutting her off.)* — Center of the universe.

JESS: Where'd you get this picture?

MAX: A real estate site, on the Internet. Help me with the blanket.

JESS: *(She does.)* But there's nothing here. I hear real estate I think condo.

MAX: *(He sits, pours her coffee from thermos.)* It's way better than a condo. Sit. *(She does.)* Have a cup of coffee. *(He hands her coffee.)* It's land, sweetie. 87 acres of it at $1,300 an acre.

JESS: So, what, you want to buy a couple acres and camp out in the cold?

MAX: Actually, I want the whole thing.

JESS: The whole thing. *(She puts coffee down.)* Eighty-seven acres.

MAX: 87 acres.

JESS: $1,300 an acre.

MAX: $1,300 an acre.

JESS: That's 7 million dollars.

MAX: $113,100.

JESS: Oh, OK, well that I have. Just take me home and I'll break open my piggy bank.

MAX: How about we both break our piggy banks? Stocks, 401(k), bonds, we can do this.

JESS: What, this? There's nothing here!

MAX: We can build a house, a homestead — a log cabin, adobe, corn cob.

JESS: You want me to live in a corn cob? Why not a peanut shell?

MAX: People do it honey; they live off-grid all the time.

JESS: Honey, there aren't even power lines out here.

MAX: Honey, that's what off-grid means.

JESS: There's no plumbing.

MAX: There's —

JESS: I am not using an outhouse!

MAX: Composting toilets.

JESS: I don't want to know.

MAX: Honey, I've been researching this for quite a while now. I didn't know how to tell you.

JESS: Composting toilet? You mean you go in it . . . and then it just sits there?

MAX: Well, I mean, there's a fan . . . on the electric one.

JESS: But we don't have electric.

MAX: Right. Well, we could get a generator.

JESS: For the composting toilet.

MAX: Well, we'll have some appliances, refrigerator —

JESS: I'm pretty sure we could leave our food outside ten months outta the year.

MAX: Well, you'd want a root cellar.

JESS: I would? Where's this coming from?

MAX: You know, that is a good question.

JESS: Thanks, I thought of it myself.

MAX: I was wondering myself where all this came from, I'm not even sure where I got the original idea.

JESS: Do you know when? 'Cuz I'd kinda like to know how long you've been planning to kidnap me and make me live in a cold corn cob with a composting toilet.

MAX: Gosh, uh, three months, maybe.

JESS: Three months!

MAX: Yeah, I guess — around Mother's Day.

JESS: Don't remind me.

MAX: Sweetie, you know she picks on you because you're a better cake decorator than she is.

JESS: I know, but she still drives me insane.

MAX: That's what bosses do. My boss too, he's a jerk.

JESS: I'll take him over her any day.

MAX: But that's my point. We shouldn't have to work for people who don't treat us right. We should work for ourselves.

JESS: You want to start a business?

MAX: No . . . I want . . . I want us to be self-sufficient, self-sustaining. Grow our own food, raise our own meat.

JESS: You want to raise meat? You mean like cows and pigs?

MAX: And chickens for eggs.

JESS: Why not turkeys?

MAX: You can't have chickens and turkeys together, the turkeys will die. They're more susceptible to chicken diseases than the chickens are.

JESS: I can't believe you know that!

MAX: We can do this. We can take control of our own destiny, our futures, our kid's futures.

JESS: Now we're having kids?

MAX: If we live up here? Hell yeah. Just think of what a great life they'll have.

JESS: Honey, I can't even think that I'd have a great life up here. It's cold in August!

MAX: We'll have a fireplace, a wood-burning stove, a pellet stove, a corn stove . . .

JESS: Wouldn't that be dangerous if we're living in a corn cob? Might set the whole place on fire.

MAX: I'm serious, Jess. I'm tired of working for other people. I want to work for me. For us. We can do this, Jess. I know we can.

JESS: Look, I can do anything I want to, I know that. I'm just not sure this is what I want.

I mean, hey, getting away from the old lady . . . I'm all for that, sign me up. But, a homestead? Homesteading? I'm not sure it's right for me, for us . . . sweetie, you just started doing the dishes a few months ago.

MAX: Right! When I got this idea . . . I wanted to prove to myself I could do it.

JESS: Honey, there's a big difference between doing the dishes and slaughtering a pig.

MAX: You can help.

JESS: I'm not slaughtering a pig. A chicken maybe — at a certain time of the month.

MAX: C'mon, just paste that old lady's face over the pigs.

JESS: She already looks like a pig *(Laughs.)* . . . no, that's not fair.

BOTH: To the pig! *(They laugh.)*

JESS: Ah, we're so good together sometimes. Let's get married.

MAX: We're already married. Let's start a new life together. Here.

JESS: Can I sleep on it?

MAX: Absolutely.

JESS: Will you actually let me sleep and not stick me in the car and take me someplace else?

MAX: Absolutely

JESS: Can I eat my pie now?

MAX: Absolutely.

JESS: Let's not talk about the composting toilet while we're eating, OK?

MAX: Deal.

(They both start to eat their pie slices.)

JESS: This is good for a supermarket pie.

MAX: Just think . . . if we live here you can make your own pie . . . from scratch. We could even grow the ingredients.

JESS: Are you out of your mind? I'll buy the crust . . . I may make the filling. *(Eats some.)* No, maybe I'll buy that too.

MAX: You're not much of a homesteader, are you?

JESS: How about I make you a mud pie and you can eat that!

MAX: You're so good to me sometimes.

JESS: I know. Now shut up and eat your pie.

MAX: Yes dear.

JESS: I love you sweetie.

MAX: Right back at ya babe.

(They eat their pie for a moment, Jess gets a better idea.)

JESS: Just in case I decide this is a good idea . . . maybe we should christen the land?

MAX: Christen it?

JESS: Yeah, isn't it an ancient Native American custom to christen the land for fertility?

MAX: Your fertility or the lands?

JESS: Maybe both.

MAX: Yes, you're right. That *is* an ancient Native American custom.

JESS: Well we'd better get to it . . . wouldn't want to piss off the natives.

MAX: Never.

(Jess leans over and kisses Max. They embrace and pull the blanket over them as the lights fade.)
(Blackout.)

END OF PLAY

PRIZE INSIDE

PETER HANRAHAN

For my parents, and for Becky.

Prize Inside was commissioned from and premiered at Mile Square Theatre (Chris O'Connor, Artistic Director), Hoboken, N.J., on June 26, 2004, for the *2nd Annual 7th Inning Stretch: 7 10-minute plays about baseball.* It was directed by Michole Biancosino. Cast: Joey — David Newer; Leila — Blair Brooks.

CHARACTERS
JOEY, a man in his fifties
LEILA, a woman in her twenties/thirties

SETTING
The seats in a baseball stadium where important people sit

• • •

A baseball stadium. The seats up front where players' wives and important guests sit. The thunder and white noise of an ongoing game are heard. Bright sunlight suggests high afternoon. Leila, a beautiful young woman, sits pensively. She wears a sunbonnet and sunglasses, and her appearance, if not her manner, should suggest Audrey Hepburn in Breakfast at Tiffany's. *She removes her sunglasses once to wipe her eyes. She's been crying. Over the noise, a rebel yell:*

JOEY: *Craaaaaacker Jaaaack! Craaaaaacker Jaaaack!* Get yer Cracker Jacks here! Right here. Cracker Jacks comin' through. Caramel-coated goodness. *When you want something sweet, and you want it now.*
(*As he hollers, Joey emerges behind Leila. The crack of a bat.*)
JOEY: *Whoo-wee!* That Jack Holloran can smack it.
LEILA: Yes. He can.
JOEY: Right into the gap. Right on in there. No way they can't catch him.
LEILA: (*Wipes her eyes.*) Nobody can.
JOEY: Nope. No, sir. You said it, lady.
LEILA: Almost everything he does, he does too fast.
JOEY: That's our Jack, for you.
LEILA: (*Removes her sunglasses.*) That's my Jack.
(*Beat.*)
JOEY: Yes, ma'am. Nothing like an afternoon game. Weekday game. Just like this. Sun like a loudspeaker up there. Hollering down.
LEILA: It's a bright one.
JOEY: You said it, lady. And, man. Smell a fresh cut grass. Hot dogs. Even sun has a smell, sort of. Doesn't it?
LEILA: I suppose so.
JOEY: Almost like nothing bad could happen to you in a place like this. (*Beat.*) Say, can I interest *you* in some Cracker Jacks?
LEILA: No, no thank you.
JOEY: You sure? Day game like this. Need something tide you over 'till dinner.

LEILA: I'm fine, thank you.

JOEY: 'Member one time, I was a kid. It was my birthday. My dad, he came, took me out a school on my birthday. Said there's a family emergency. I got all worked up wondering what's the emergency.

(Leila takes a cell phone out of her purse.)

LEILA: If you'll excuse me, I'm waiting for a call.

JOEY: Oh. *Oh.* Don't mean to bother you. Just about to say. Only emergency my family ever had was *baseball. (Beat.)* You all right? You're lookin' a little peaked just now.

LEILA: Long morning. And this heat.

JOEY: Ain't the heat, but the humidity that does it.

LEILA: I don't mean to be rude, but — are vendors *allowed* in this area?

JOEY: You betcha. Got the run a the park. But I'm bothering you?

LEILA: It's all right. If you'll just —

JOEY: Guess I got so wrapped up in the game, I just ambled on down here, started yakking. Please accept my apologies.

LEILA: There's no need to apologize. But I'd like to get back to the game. And my phone call —

(The crack of a bat.)

JOEY: Oh! Oh! Is it — ? *Almost.*

(A chorus of disappointed "Aws" and "Ohs.")

JOEY: *Say.* This where all the players' wives sit, huh? And girlfriends. And kids. And best, good friends. Huh? Isn't it? Didn't even notice.

LEILA: Who's on deck, can you see?

JOEY: Don't know. But, man, Holloran's looking kinda itchy out there. Think he's going to steal? I seen him do it.

LEILA: *(Upset.)* So have I.

JOEY: Sure I can't offer you some Cracker Jack? As a consolation for trespassing my way over here?

LEILA: No, thank you. Really.

JOEY: Bet you didn't know Cracker Jack's over one hundred years old.

LEILA: No, I did not.

JOEY: Yes, ma'am. Introduced to the world in the Year of Our Lord eighteen-hundred and ninety-three. Columbia Exposition. That's the Chicago World's fair. But it goes back way before that.

LEILA: *Does it?*

JOEY: Bet you didn't know the Indians. I mean, the Native Americans. Used to make popcorn, pour molasses all over it, keep it fresh, make it sweet.

LEILA: No, I didn't know that.

JOEY: That's over one thousand years ago they were doing that. AD 500 or 800 or something. So, you think about it. Cracker Jack's older even than the United States. Just a little bit younger than Jesus.

LEILA: I guess that's right.

JOEY: Bet you didn't know Cracker Jack used to mean "awesome." Imagine that, people walking down the street saying, "Man, that's so *cracker jack.*"

LEILA: Imagine that.

JOEY: Bet you didn't know I'm the number-three Cracker Jack vendor in the whole country.

LEILA: Are you? Congratulations. But my phone call —

JOEY: Now, they first started putting prizes in your Cracker Jack boxes round about 1912. So, you know that movie, *Breakfast at Tiffany's?*

LEILA: I've seen it, yes.

JOEY: Where they find a ring in the box, take it to Tiffany's, have it engraved?

LEILA: I remember that. I know the whole film . . . by heart.

JOEY: That's actually anomalous cause they stopped using metal to make the prizes during World War II. Good scene, though. Fella at Tiffany's, the jeweler, says, "Do they still really have prizes in Cracker Jack boxes?" And George Peppard, he says, "*Oh, yes.*" Just like that. And the jeweler, he says, "That's nice to know — "

LEILA: "It gives one a feeling of solidarity almost, of continuity with the past, that sort of thing."

JOEY: That sort of thing, yes ma'am.

LEILA: I'm afraid I don't know about that sort of thing.

JOEY: How do you mean?

LEILA: I gave up my past for someone else's future.

JOEY: Like I always say, if we could see the future, we wouldn't need baseball. *Say.* You ain't the wife of one a 'em, are you?

LEILA: No, no. Not exactly. Not yet, is what I mean to say.

JOEY: What's that mean, not yet? Girlfriend?

LEILA: Sort of.

JOEY: Seen a lot a girlfriends come and go. Which one is he?

LEILA: Jack.

JOEY: Holloran? *No kidding.*

LEILA: Why do you say that?

JOEY: What? What'd I say?

LEILA: No kidding. Like that. Like you said it.

JOEY: I didn't mean nothing by it. I just . . . uh . . . heard things, you know.

LEILA: What things?

JOEY: Just things. Around. Like people do. Like he's sort of a — uh —

LEILA: What?

JOEY: A, well, tomcat, I guess you'd say.

LEILA: Yes. So they say. And I didn't believe them, but —

JOEY: But you're together six years. And you're not going nowhere apparently. And he hasn't popped the question. So —

LEILA: *So.*

JOEY: I'm Joey, by the way. But they call me Number Three.

LEILA: Because you're the number three —

JOEY: Cause I'm the number-three Cracker Jack vendor in the U. S. of A.

LEILA: I'm Leila.

(*Joey takes a seat next to Leila.*)

JOEY: *I know who you are.* I didn't want to say. But I got a bet going with Number Two. (*Gestures to the bleachers.*) If you squint, you can see him up there in the cheap seats.

LEILA: Where?

JOEY: There. Big, fat white guy. Glandular condition.

LEILA: Oh. I see.

JOEY: That's where all your big numbers are. Nosebleed section. But I got a bet going, says I can sell you a box a Cracker Jacks. No questions asked. And that you'll actually open 'em up and eat 'em.

LEILA: Oh, I don't know.

JOEY: 'Cause the players' wives and girlfriends never eat a thing. Not a morsel. You're the Holy Grail. Nobody's never sold nothing to you. And here's the kicker. In a couple a months, they're switching to Crunch 'n' Munch. So what do you say?

LEILA: I'm sorry. I don't think I can. Not right now. I'm not feeling well.

JOEY: Is it the humidity? It's the humidity. I'll go and get you a *sody.*

LEILA: It's not — the humidity.

JOEY: Not the humidity? Then what?

(*The crack of a bat.*)

JOEY: *Whoop.* Watch out! Gets me every time.

LEILA: Me too.

JOEY: Little mid-air heart attack.

LEILA: The truth is, Joey. *Number Three.* Jack and I. (*Whisper.*) We've been having trouble.

JOEY: *What?* Why? Everybody says you're perfect. Got your pictures on magazines. And you're always *smiling.* Doublewide grin big as the day is long.

LEILA: You never can tell what's behind a smile.

JOEY: What's the trouble?

LEILA: Well, we were happy.

JOEY: Uh-huh.

LEILA: For a long time.

JOEY: I get you.

LEILA: But it's been a long time, you see. *(Beat.)* Before we met, I was going to be an actress.

JOEY: Oh, one of those.

LEILA: It's what kept me up nights when I was a girl — imagining myself as someone else. All glittering and different. And I landed a part, I did. A good one. *(Beat.)* Then I met Jack.

JOEY: Then you met Jack.

LEILA: Tell me, Joey, is it possible to become addicted to a *person?* I gave up everything. He didn't ask me to, but I did. And now. It's been six years.

JOEY: So you're getting a little impatient, is it?

LEILA: You could say.

JOEY: Wanting to settle down for good, kind of like?

LEILA: *Yes.* But Jack's so — so —

JOEY: Kinda like a fly ball you can't see cause a the sun, but you know it's up there. And you're squinting and squirming and moving around and just hoping like hell it lands in your glove?

LEILA: He didn't come home last night. He left a message, saying he'd call from the dugout. But he hasn't called.

JOEY: Oh, I know the type. I sure do. Wait! He's going for it!

LEILA: He's stealing?

(Leila and Joey stand.)

JOEY: Heading home! He's going. He's got it! He's right on it!

LEILA: Safe! He's — *safe.*

JOEY: What a madman. Goddamn madman. *(Beat.)* Look at that. You see that? He looked right at ya.

(Leila and Joey sit.)

LEILA: Did he?

JOEY: You didn't see?

LEILA: I don't think so, no.

JOEY: Right at you, Leila. Nowhere else. The eyes of a man in love, if I ever seen 'em.

LEILA: You think?

JOEY: I know.

(Joey stands.)

JOEY: I been married twenty-one years. I got the same identical eyes. And you know what my wife says. She says, you got to keep your eyes on the prize. Just like a box of Cracker Jacks. Everybody's got a prize inside. Sometimes it's right on top, first thing you see. Other times, you got to dig down deep, all the way to the bottom.

LEILA: He's waving to me.

JOEY: Wave back, already.

(*Leila waves.*)

JOEY: Now, you ask me. He's just biding his time. Any day, now, Leila. Any day.

LEILA: Do you really think?

JOEY: Like I said, *I know.*

LEILA: Yes, you do know, don't you?

JOEY: Now, can I interest you in a box of Cracker Jacks? Prize inside.

(*Beat.*)

LEILA: Do they . . . still really have prizes in Cracker Jack boxes?

JOEY: *Oh, yes.*

LEILA: How much?

JOEY: Three dollars, ma'am.

(*Leila fingers through her purse, hands him cash.*)

JOEY: Thank you, Leila.

LEILA: Thank you, Number Three.

(*Joey heads off, the way he came.*)

JOEY: *Craaaaaacker Jaaaack! Craaaaaacker Jaaaack!* Get yer Cracker Jacks here! *When you want something sweet, and you want it now!*

(*Leila opens the box of Cracker Jack. She peers in. She shakes the box. She sticks her hand in. She digs all the way to the bottom. She shakes again. She shakes more and more frantically. She empties the contents of the box. There is no prize. She stands slowly, dons her sunglasses, leaves the cell phone on the seat, and exits. The second verse of "Moon River" swells: Two drifters off to see the world/There's such a lot of world to see . . . The cell phone rings.*)

END OF PLAY

THE REMOTE

Mark Harvey Levine

The Remote was first produced by Company Of Angels (Los Angeles, California) in April 1999. It was directed by Wendy Worthington, with the following cast: Alma — Sarah Nina Phillips; Sam — Mark Harvey Levine. *The Remote* had its first Equity production as part of *Cabfare for the Common Man* at The Phoenix Theatre (Indianapolis, In.) in May 2005. Bryan D. Fonseca was the artistic director. It was directed by Bryan D. Fonseca, with the following cast: Alma — Sara Rieman; Sam — Michael Shelton.

CHARACTERS

ALMA, thirties to forties, currently looking a little tired
SAM, thirties to forties, currently looking even more tired

SETTING

Alma and Sam's living room. A couch and an overstuffed chair face the
TV, which is offstage toward the audience.

• • •

*The living room of a nice, but by no means fancy, apartment. Alma and Sam
are sprawled out on a big chair and the couch. Wrappers from eaten fast food
are nearby. We hear the TV softly playing. Alma and Sam look like they're
dead, but in fact they're watching TV, the blue light flickering on their
zombie-like faces. Perhaps they drool. Finally Alma stirs.*

ALMA: Uhmm . . . urmn . . . Sam . . . Sam . . . we gotta go to bed . . .
   (Sam grunts.)
ALMA: *(Continued.)* *(Looking at her watch.)* My God . . . it's already tomor-
   row . . . Come on. Shut the damn thing off.
   (She doesn't get up.)
SAM: 'Kay . . . Just once more around the channels . . .
   (Sam, using the remote, starts "flipping" through the channels.)
ALMA: I hate when you do this. OK . . . this is it . . . I'm really getting
   up . . . I'm gonna put the dishes in the machine . . .
   (Groggily, she stands and exits to the kitchen. We hear vague dish sounds.)
SAM: *(Still flipping.)* Ahhh . . . trash, trash, *(Stunned by something.)* dear
   God . . . trash, garbage, trash, awful, awful . . .
ALMA: *(Offstage.)* Sam, c'mon . . . turn it off and come to bed.
SAM: OK.
   *(He points the remote at the TV. There is a blinding flash of light. Sam reacts
   as if he's been struck by lightning. The TV goes dark and quiet but the signal
   goes "into" Sam.)*
SAM: *(Commercial.)* "— your local dealership."
   "I thought it was *your* turn to buy the groceries."
   "Galapagos . . . Island of mystery."
ALMA: *(Offstage.)* *(Overlapping.)* Sam? C'mon, turn the TV off . . .
   (His eyes frightened, he tries to call to her but it comes out as television.)
SAM: "Into the low 50s"
   "They sent five men in. None returned"

"La pierna! Oh, la pierna"

"In a prepared statement today — "

(Alma reenters, wiping her hands with a dish-towel.)

ALMA: Sam, you want to come to —

(She reacts to the TV shows pouring forth from Sam.)

Sam? Honey?

Oh my God . . . what's wrong with you?! Sam? What's going on?

SAM: "with sixteen prior arrests"

"been using it for years!"

"Ahhhh . . . adverb trouble"

"How's life treatin' you, Norm?"

"brings you this report on Swiss — "

"Oh, you would think that."

(Explosion.)

"This, I believe, is where we run"

"Seven men. On horseback."

(Sam, still spouting TV, mimes what happened: He pointed the remote at the TV, and the signal seems to have jumped inside him.)

ALMA: Stop! Stop! Sam, make it stop!

SAM: "when the Germans advanced toward Lausanne"

(Sam gestures with his hands — he doesn't know how to stop it.)

ALMA: Here — Here, drink something!

(She hands him a drink from the table.)

SAM: "In Albuquerque, for the next three weeks"

"WHAT were you thinking?"

"lemme 'splain it to you"

"—may be different with each individual cat"

(Sam drinks. We hear the TV gurgling through the water. A lot of it spills down his shirt.)

(She shakes him violently. Some shaky TV still manages to escape. He glares at her.)

ALMA: I'm sorry! I'm sorry! I don't know what to do! You've never spouted television before! What do I do? What do I do?

SAM: "And Rhonda, your husband is here with us?"

(Blues song:.) "Well, I woke up this morning"

(Sam makes the hand sign for "remote.")

ALMA: . . . The remote! Ahhh, that's the spot.

SAM: "They'll take out your gall bladder, but they won't take — "

"Well, it's one small step — "

(Alma grabs the remote, tries pointing it at the TV — nothing. Alma points

the remote at Sam and now Alma reacts as if she's been zapped by electricity. Sam falls silent, and Alma picks up in mid-sentence where he left off.)

ALMA: "—for a man, one giant leap for — "

"wouldn't you like to come away?"

(Applause.)

"with a five inch heel"

"you take the car, and then you "

"kick it along side, laterally, through"

"a low pressure zone coming in from Seattle"

"which should bring prices down"

"were gonna be a boy, this area here would be, like, off the page —"

"I'm awake, I'm awake!"

"full of earthy, crunchy goodness"

"Just dial 10-10-666, then 1, then —"

(After a moment's stunned pause.)

SAM: What the hell was that?! That was the most bizarre thing I've ever — It's like I was . . . Alma? Alma?! Oh, God, now you've got it. Alma! Alma! Listen to me . . . I know you can hear me . . . I'm going to figure this out . . . just hang in there . . .

(Alma nods as she gushes TV.)

ALMA: "can I call you Nigel? You look like a Nigel"

"Ik beno sgrupo alongpe, nakto plah"

(Galloping horses sound.)

"this, then, is where the wildebeests-"

(Grandiose music.)

"for only $19.95 you get the flange, the gramplet *and* the"

SAM: I'll call the paramedics *(Starts to leave.)* What am I going to tell them, my wife is receiving television signals through her head? No one's going to believe this — I don't believe this . . .

ALMA: "A low pressure system coming in from the East"

"It's on the Lido deck! Hurry!"

(Electronic music.)

"I don't care where you eat!"

"Someone tried to kill Asa!"

"If it's not . . . I mean, if it's really"

(She shoots an exasperated look at him.)

"And that's your testimony?"

"In this series last season, with the Gators taking the lead"

SAM: Hang on Honey — I'll think of something — I don't know what, but —

(Pause.)

SAM: HOW THE HELL AM I SUPPOSED TO THINK WITH THE TV ALWAYS ON!!!

Dammit! Look, I can't stand to see you like that. Let me — let me see if I can take it back.

(He grabs the remote, points it at her, and the TV switches back into him.)

ALMA: My God! That was the weirdest sensation! It was like watching every TV show at once. News from Romania! Wrestling! Old sitcoms, game shows, a really great recipe for low-fat Lemon Chicken, actually —

SAM: "Step into the car, sir"

"And the so-called White Man"

"Screamed like a woman"

"Up 15% over last week, with an index of"

"Tomorrow? Tomorrow I'll be gone."

" . . . Ouch! . . . "

"but my mama was a go-go girl"

(Sam waves his arms to get her back on track.)

ALMA: I know, I know. It's just — I just can't get over it. All that information. And entertainment. And pure dreck. Like having all of humanity wash over you.

SAM: "Hey! I'm talking now!"

"Your free gift if you respond within seven days"

"Forceps . . . .three oh two silk . . . "

"Wait . . . you say it was your mother"

"Huh? You know what I mean? Huh?"

"The latest smash hit from the Elastic Pressband"

(Sam looks exasperated at her.)

ALMA: What do you expect me to do? Sam? Is this some sort of punishment? Is God angry at us? Is the cable company angry at us? *(To the heavens.)* Whatever I did, I'm sorry, already! Alright?!

You . . . want me to take it? OK. OK.

SAM: "It's the Frogs' ball, third down, on the Pittsburgh 25"

"For a limited time only!"

"Zombies?" "I'm afraid so"

"The environment's in shambles"

"Over twenty-five tribes of California Indians are joining me in supporting—"

(Sam motions to her to take the remote.)

SAM: "It's unimaginable that you'd have a report on this"

"I feel like I've been shut out of your life"

"I'm gonna put the dishes in the machine"

(She scrunches her eyes, hits the remote, and gets the TV back into her.)

ALMA: "They say there are tigers in these parts"

"A tribute to warrior faith and virtue"

"But it's not . . . the thing is, it's not — "

"Have you ever seen calcium that goes this way?"

"We're back with noted author Hildegarde—"

(Eerie music.)

"Precision engineered with real Bolivian craftsmanship"

"Fourth down, and I don't think they can pass it"

"No, wait — you said it was your sister?"

SAM: . . . Yes! Just for a second. Now listen. God is not punishing us. We haven't done anything wrong. And anyway, God does not let people starve in Africa, but then suddenly look over and say "Hey, the Sobels are watching too much TV, I better screw with their minds for a little bit!" I won't believe that. There has to be some kind of perfectly reasonable, scientific explanation. And that's what you have to find out.

(And with that, he takes the remote and gets the TV back into him.)

ALMA: What?! WHAT?! Oh, sure! No problem! How the heck am I supposed to do that!!! You always do this! Whenever's there's a problem you just leave it with me. I mean, yes, it's nice that I've learned a little spot plumbing and how to rewire a doorbell but I'd love it if you did a few things, too. Y'know. Even if it was the dishes, or the odd exorcism here or there, like when one of us is possessed with the spirit of television.

SAM: "If you watch closely, you can see the baby camel take it's first steps"

"But the American people — if you'll let me finish, Senator — the American people —"

"Are you familiar with the one they call . . . Nosferatu?"

"Yeah . . . I'll hold the ball and you run and kick it!"

"Oh no! Charlie's got the bag! And it's in his locker!"

(Battle sounds.)

"When the San Francisco Giants take on the New York Jets"

"Exploring the art of big screen illusion"

"I must say, you look particularly beautiful this fine evening".

"Woah . . . I think I'm in trouble!"

(She watches Sam for a little bit.)

ALMA: Y'know, this is almost like actually watching TV.

SAM: "It's not pink, it's salmon"

"It's you! You're here! This is great!"

(Sam coughs, and she taps Sam gently on the sides, like a misbehaving TV set.)

ALMA: Oh my God, I think I recognized that commercial. Sam! SAM! I know that commercial. From years ago. It's in my head, too! How do I turn it off?! How do I turn it off?!

SAM: "Fortified with important vitamins!"

"Hey, the Fonz is buried up to his waist in dirt!"

"the president of the United States is"

"Sarah! You?! How can it be?"

(Dixieland music.)

"It's the cheese."

"Till we get to see each other again!"

"Using her powerful jaws, the female rips open her prey."

(Sam makes protesting gestures. He hands her the remote. She hits the button . . .)

ALMA: "Book 'em"

"And den ya add da oregeno! Did ya see that? Did you see what I did there?"

"And now here's Phil with the weather."

"A kick here, a punch there, a twist, a dodge, a flip"

SAM: Look, I dunno how this happened but . . . we'll get out of this, Honey, together. Just like we . . . just like we . . . I'm sure we've done something together . . .

(He takes the remote back. Switch. They continue to switch, handing the remote back and forth.)

ALMA: The only thing we do together is come home every single night and zone out in front of the TV! Why aren't we "going and doing"?! Let's just go out. See a movie, see a play, for God's sakes. Alright, nobody goes to see plays, but still. Something! My God, look at the ideas I'm coming up with. If we're not watching TV I've got us watching movies. Sam! Why are we doing this?

SAM: "The head waiter, he will want to apologize to you himself."

"Wasn't it great seeing everybody?"

"you know I hate to tell you this, but it's time to defrost that freezer"

"More wine anyone? Yeah. I'll take some."

"Pandolfo didn't wait long to put the Devils ahead, sweeping a rebound past Richter at 3:40 of the first period"

"Bears? Bears?! There's not supposed to be Bears."

ALMA: "Get the trajectory termination as soon as possible!"

"for the second straight night Thursday and Iraqis dug in"

"The mega-sale is store wide! Friday 8 AM till midnite, and Saturday 10 AM till midnight"

"How many legs? How many legs?"

"I'm gonna belt you, grandpa."

"When you bring home a plate of nachos, smothered with cheese "

"I have deleted the appropriate program."

SAM: How should I know? All I know is, at the end of a day I like to watch a little TV! When I'm at work, I have to be "on" all the time, you know? I have to say stuff like "Would you like to see our selection of hand-finished Italian made range hoods?" I hate being "on." When I come home, I want to be "off."

ALMA: Well, we're sure "off," now, Sam. We're all the way off. When did this happen, Sam? How did this happen? We don't do anything anymore, we just watch other people do things on TV.

SAM: "Here's a man who's written more than thirty books . . . "

"Hello?? Hello?? Stupid cordless phone!"

"You can follow some vague recipe for box office success as closely as you want"

ALMA: "You can race 'em! Or loop the loop!"

"the 30s in the Northeast and Ohio Valley; the 40s in the mid-Atlantic, Midwest and mountain"

"It's that time of the year again. Confused? Don't be."

"also will feature drive time radio ads and online advertisements on major Internet sites that will"

"Tired of cooking? Tired of cleaning?"

SAM: I dunno . . . .It's just that, y'know . . . the people on TV are . . . Smarter. Funnier. Better looking. Let's face it, they're more interesting than we are. Than I am. I mean, that's really it, isn't it? I bore you! I don't have . . . y'know, whiter teeth, fresher breath, leather seats . . .

ALMA: We could be having those lives, too, Sam. You want a sitcom? Fine! Remember we used to laugh together? God, you used to make me laugh. I used to start wheezing, I was laughing so hard. How about romance? Adventure? Intrigue!

SAM: "A full service day-spa, with all the amenities"

(Sung.) "And you are just as special as special can be"

"Oil and gas tax breaks alone account for close to $11 billion."

"Save on sweaters, jeans, knits and all housewares"

"well I don't need much, just three squares will do it"

ALMA: "Get your friends. Have a party. And let the good times roll."

"I feel like a tuna on toast sandwich"

"It's the perfect way to renew old acquaintances."

"I heard everything you said!"

SAM: And when are we going to do all this? We're already exhausted! We come home, and if we're lucky we have enough energy to microwave dinner before we fall over!

ALMA: We have to. We have to. Otherwise we may as well give up, and admit we're strangers to each other.

SAM: "The ultimate entertainment destination"

"Low pressure pushing through the eastern Great Lakes Thursday"

ALMA: "My experience was good, because . . . they treat me like a king"

SAM: What, strangers? We're not strangers.

ALMA: We've drifted apart. We're the remote ones. We've become remote from each other.

SAM: "I'm here about the nanny job. I'll keep a watchful eye on your kids"

"I think you'll be pleased with these rosebushes."

ALMA: "An impressionistic view of Rome, spanning forty years"

SAM: What?

(Alma gets a little annoyed at his one-word response.)

ALMA: We don't know each other anymore. We know the people on *West Wing* better than each other.

SAM: "The hottest spot in the continental United States on Wednesday was"

"Here's a, poem that I like, particularly.

ALMA: "Week after week the survey proves"

"Discover the music."

"Voiceprint identification positive"

SAM: I know you! I know what you're thinking! And I know you're bored with me!

ALMA: And I know you're not attracted to me anymore! With 100 percent fruit juice, and all the vitamin C your child needs.

(Pause before she takes the remote again.)

ALMA: "New kissable lipstick"

SAM: What?!? That's ridiculous!

ALMA: It's true and you know it.

SAM: "that stays on your lips and not — "

ALMA: "in your wardrobe"

SAM: You're beautiful!

ALMA: I am not.

SAM: "With soft, silky manageable"

ALMA: Quick, Tiffany, run!"

SAM: You are too!

ALMA: I'm ugly.

SAM: "Looking for wild girls?"

ALMA: "For the sexiest live talk—"

SAM: You're gorgeous!

ALMA: I'm fat.

SAM: "With smooth, creamy"

ALMA: "The Fashion Award goes to"

SAM: You're sexy!

ALMA: I'm old.

SAM: "My blouse! It's all wet!"

ALMA: "With taut, firm thighs and a"

SAM: You're crazy!

ALMA: It's true.

SAM: "Two piece, french-cut"

ALMA: " — flat, washboard stomach"

SAM: Who ever told you you were ugly?

ALMA: *(Points at TV.)* He did!

SAM: "supple curves"

> *(He grabs the remote but instead of switching, he kisses her. Still kissing, they both open their eyes — realizing that for the first time since Sam was zapped, there's silence. Finally, they part.)*

SAM: Wow . . . quiet.

ALMA: I'd forgotten what it was like.

SAM: It's nice.

ALMA: We should get quiet more often.

SAM: We should talk more often.

ALMA: . . . We'll talk quietly.

SAM: And then sometimes we won't talk.

ALMA: We'll just stare at each other?

SAM: I like looking at you.

ALMA: I like looking at you, too.

> *(They look at each other for a second. Then they look at the TV).*

ALMA: *(Continued.)* Let's never turn the damn thing on again.

SAM: *(Re: the remote.)* What'll we do with this? Hang on — I'll solve this one.
> *(He tries to snap the remote in half. But it won't break.)*

SAM: No, wait, wait. *(He wraps remote in the towel.)* OK, Mrs. Sobel?

ALMA: All right, Mr. Sobel.

SAM: This concludes our broadcasting day.

> *(As in a Jewish wedding, he places the wrapped remote at their feet and steps on it. They kiss. Blackout.)*

END OF PLAY

RIGHT SENSATION

RICH ORLOFF

Right Sensation was originally produced in April, 2004, in the
"Just Add Water" Festival produced by the WorkShop Theater
Company in New York City. The cast included Tracy Newirth
and David Walters, and the play was directed by Holli Harms.
Right Sensation was produced in May, 2007, as part of Rich
Orloff's *Couples*, produced by the WorkShop Theater Company
in New York City. The cast included Michael Anderson and
Jacqueline M. Raposo, and the play was directed by
Paula D'Alessandris.

CHARACTERS
PAULA, thirties to forties
STEWART, thirties to forties

PLACE
Paula's bedroom

TIME
Evening

· · ·

As the play begins, Paula and Stewart are in Paula's bedroom, kissing with enthusiasm. They're horny and attracted to each other, but they are not yet comfortable and confident with each other. They're both dressed and have not yet reached the bed.

PAULA: You kiss really well.
STEWART: Thanks. You, too.
PAULA: And I'm not just saying that because I'm drunk.
STEWART: Me, neither.
PAULA: I'm not that drunk.
STEWART: I'm as drunk or as not drunk as you want me to be.
   (He puts his hand up her blouse. She moves it away from her breasts, and so he slides it to the back of her blouse. They continue to kiss.)
PAULA: I don't normally do this.
STEWART: Me, neither.
PAULA: I've never done this.
STEWART: I'm willing to have done this or not done this, whichever you prefer.
   (She moves his hand away from her bra strap. They continue kissing, and his hand moves to the bra strap again.)
PAULA: Please don't.
STEWART: OK.
   (Their kissing becomes more passionate. Stewart puts a hand on her bra strap and quickly unsnaps it. Paula recoils, grabbing her blouse so her bra stays on.)
PAULA: I said NO, you bastard!
   (Paula runs into her bathroom and slams the door. Stewart is a bit stunned. He approaches the door.)
STEWART: Look, I'm, I'm, I'm sorry, I — I didn't mean to, it's just — when my

hand gets in the vicinity . . . I, I can't tell you how proud I was when I mastered the skill . . . I'm, I'm really sorry . . . Patty, are you OK?

PAULA: *(Offstage.) (Not OK.)* I'm fine, and my name's Paula.

STEWART: Will you come out — Paula . . . please?

PAULA: Why should I?

STEWART: 'Cause, 'cause I'd like to see you.

PAULA: Why?

STEWART: Because, because you're nice, and, and you're really sexy, and you have a great smile.

PAULA: What if I didn't have teeth?

STEWART: You'd still be sexy.

PAULA: Why?

STEWART: Well, you have beautiful eyes.

PAULA: What if I didn't have eyes?

STEWART: You'd still be sexy.

PAULA: Why?

STEWART: You have a great neck.

PAULA: What if I didn't have a neck?

STEWART: Is this a puzzle? Because I suck at puzzles. You want to torture me? Lock me in a room with a crossword puzzle.

(Paula enters.)

PAULA: What if I only had one breast?

STEWART: I see two . . . don't I?

PAULA: I had a mastectomy.

STEWART: Oh . . . Oh, well, you know, that's OK, no, I mean it's not O — I mean, whatever . . . So you had cancer?

PAULA: No, my right breast just got in the way during archery.

STEWART: I'm sorry, I was —

PAULA: No, no, that's —

STEWART: They look fine. From here.

PAULA: I had an implant.

(A long silence.)

PAULA: *(Continued.)* If you want to go . . .

STEWART: No, I, I, I just can't think of anything to say that doesn't make me sound like a jerk. Which I'm not, I swear, I'm not, it's just not always readily apparent.

PAULA: You don't seem like a jerk.

STEWART: Yeah, well, the night is young. How long ago did —

PAULA: Uhhhhh while ago.

STEWART: Am I your —

PAULA: Uh-huh.

STEWART: How much did you have to drink to —

PAULA: I didn't count.

STEWART: Well, I'm honored you chose me.

PAULA: You should be.

STEWART: You know, you really don't have to be self-conscious, I mean, I've seen implants before.

PAULA: You have?

STEWART: Sure. Plenty of times.

PAULA: Plenty of times?

STEWART: After my divorce, I uh, I uh, I kind of went through a, a strip joint phase — which I'm *way* over —

PAULA: Uh-huh.

STEWART: Anyway, so, like shifting subjects, like I know this must be traumatic but, well, like what's the big deal?

PAULA: What's the — !

STEWART: I just mean, lots of people have fake parts these days. Like hip replacements, or fake knees, or hair plugs. Most people are not 100 percent there — if you know what I mean.

PAULA: It's just not the same as it was. It's like replacing, ummm —

STEWART: A Lexus with a Honda?

PAULA: No!

STEWART: *(Defensive.)* Sorry. Just trying to empathize.

PAULA: It's like replacing an orange, with a wax orange.

STEWART: Better than a wax prune.

(Off her glare:)

You know, you don't cheer up easily.

PAULA: How would you like it if you had surgery and woke up with a wax testicle?

STEWART: My trousers would be more comfortable.

Look, I'm sorry about your, your misfortune and everything, but you still got one good one, don't you? . . . Was that a stupid thing to say?

PAULA: For a human being, yes. For a guy, not necessarily.

STEWART: Look, I don't know what you — I just want to —

I, I, I've had some moles removed . . .

Not that I'm equating.

PAULA: I probably shouldn't have —

STEWART: No, no, you did the —

PAULA: It's just that, it was my favorite one.

STEWART: You had a favorite breast?

PAULA: Yes, I did.

STEWART: Why?

PAULA: It was rounder and, and perkier.

STEWART: And your other one?

PAULA: It's, it's — none of your business.

STEWART: Fine.

PAULA: I just liked my right one better.

STEWART: OK.

PAULA: Women often prefer one over the other.

STEWART: Do you have a favorite ear?

Do you prefer one nostril?

PAULA: Do you have a favorite testicle?

STEWART: I just thank God I have two . . . Oh, shit,

I mean, I'd thank God if I had one also.

PAULA: Probably not with the same gusto.

STEWART: I'm just grateful I'm not a eunuch . . . most days.

PAULA: Look, Steven, I just —

STEWART: Stewart.

PAULA: It has no nipple.

STEWART: I think nipples are highly overrated.

PAULA: You do?

STEWART: Well, starting now.

PAULA: Look, *Stewart,* I really liked kissing you —

STEWART: Same here.

PAULA: It's, you see, when I had my mastectomy, well, I thought if I had an implant, you see the doctors warned me, because of where my cancer was located, they — they had to take the nerves out with the breast. So there's not just no nipple, there's no sensation there. None.

STEWART: Nothing?

PAULA: You can touch it and lick it and put pins in it, and it feels . . . nothing.

STEWART: Oh.

PAULA: I, I wasn't going to say anything, but, but then I thought, what if he starts sucking on it, and I don't respond, and he'll think —

STEWART: It's OK.

PAULA: I mean, it's there, but don't waste your time on it.

STEWART: Does it affect your balance?

PAULA: What?

STEWART: Like you told me you like to swim. Does it affect your stroke?

PAULA: They don't weigh that much.

STEWART: Well, I've never weighed one.

PAULA: Look —

STEWART: Guys have a lot of fixations about breasts, but weighing them is not one of them.

PAULA: And what fixations *do* you have about breasts?

STEWART: Well, you know, the normal ones.

PAULA: Do you prefer them big or small?

STEWART: I've never been with a breast that's either too big *or* too small.

PAULA: Never?

STEWART: Mostly I'm just glad when they're . . . available.

PAULA: Well, one of mine isn't really available.

STEWART: That's — You know, you never asked how *many* I prefer.

PAULA: How many do you prefer?

STEWART: Five. So you're four short; live with it.

PAULA: *(Not amused.)* Thanks.

STEWART: Listen. I can see why this would be hard for you and why you had to get sloshed and all that —

PAULA: I wasn't sloshed.

STEWART: It's just — I don't care if your right boob is made of plastic, Formica, recycled linoleum, used tires, or filled vacuum cleaner bags. I like you. I find you attractive. I would like to fondle any and all of you. If you like me, you're welcome to do the same. If you don't like me, fine. But if you *do* like me, and you don't — enjoy me because you're afraid, well, well, well like now we're talking loss.

(A moment, then:)

This is about as articulate as I ever get, so don't expect better.

PAULA: What if, what if you touch it and go "ugh"?

STEWART: Then I'm a real loser.

PAULA: What if, what if you like it better than my real one?

STEWART: Then, then you can write a thank-you note to your surgeon.

PAULA: What if, what if after all this, I give in and you decide I'm a lousy lover?

STEWART: I'm not that picky.

PAULA: And what if I decide *you're* a lousy lover?

STEWART: I'll add you to the list.

PAULA: What if, what if, what if we find out we really like each other?

(A long beat.)

STEWART: Well that sobered me up. How about you?

PAULA: It's like I just drank a double espresso.

STEWART: If um, we don't have to —

PAULA: You know, about a month after the operation, I uh I decided — I — how to put this delicately —

STEWART: I'll be more turned on if you don't.

PAULA: I decided it was, it was time to "own" my sexuality again.

STEWART: Before that were you just renting?

PAULA: *So* one night I took a warm bath, with bubbles, and candles, and a glass of sherry, and I relaxed. And I came into my bedroom, and I lit some more candles, scented candles, and I got into bed, and I began to caress myself. Slowly. Delicately. Skillfully. But, but every time I touched my right breast, it was, it was as if, instead of candles, someone was shining a thousand harsh, cold fluorescent lights on me. And, and I tried to, to close my eyes and get into it again, but every, every time I touched — . . . the lights went through my eyelids.

STEWART: *(Warmly.)* Hey . . .

PAULA: *(Near tears by now.)* And if I focused on *not* touching my right breast, the lights they still —

STEWART: It's OK.

PAULA: *No, it's not.*

STEWART: Of course not, but, but — look, I haven't had the light thing –

PAULA: Then don't —

STEWART: With me it's noise. Nights when all I want to do is be with a woman, you know — I don't mean sex. I don't mean not sex, I just mean — be with her, you know? And then the noise starts. And nothing I do adjusts the volume. And soon I'm with the noise more than with the woman.

PAULA: And what do you do when that happens?

STEWART: I do what any guy would do. I beat myself up.

PAULA: And what if I, what if I do something like that while you're here?

STEWART: I dunno . . . I'll, I'll try to dim the lights for you.

(A beat.)

PAULA: I got new sheets. Do you like 'em?

STEWART: I can't tell from this far away.

(They move to the bed.)

PAULA: If we could just kiss and not —

STEWART: Whatever.

(They resume kissing. Stewart doesn't know what to do with his hands. Eventually he just sticks his arms out to his sides.)

PAULA: Oh, hell . . . Give me your hand.

(Paula takes one of Stewart's hands and places it on her right breast. Tears well up in her eyes.)

STEWART: I thought you said it had no sensation.

PAULA: Shhh.

(She leaves his hand there, and just absorbs for a moment. Then they kiss again. It's slower now and more intimate. The lights fade.)

END OF PLAY

A RUSH OF WINGS

Mrinalini Kamath

A Rush of Wings was first performed on February 27, 2007, at
the Ensemble Studio Theatre in New York City as
Night I of the Ma-Yi/Youngblood Mashup. It was directed by
Michael Lew. Cast: Emilie — Candace Thompson;
Ishmael — Debargo Sanyal.

CHARACTERS
EMILIE, female, twenties or thirties, inquisitive, curious
ISHMAEL, male, twenties or thirties, very matter-of-fact

SETTING
Their bedroom

TIME
The present, the wee hours of the morning

• • •

Setting: Queen-sized bed on a dark stage. We hear the beating of birds' wings, soft at first, but they quickly become louder. Just as they become very loud, the sound stops simultaneous with a light coming up on one figure in the bed, Emilie. She sits bolt upright, breathing hard. Ishmael, lying next to her, rolls over and awakens.

ISHMAEL: What, what's the matter? Is it your heart? Your appendix? Your —
EMILIE: A dream. I had a really . . . strange, dream.
ISHMAEL: Oh.
    (He settles himself back into the bed, turning over to go back to sleep).
    That's just your mind — you can control THAT.
EMILIE: You can?
ISHMAEL: Better than your appendix or your heart.
EMILIE: What was it about?
ISHMAEL: Huh?
EMILIE: No, I just . . . I'm wondering what my dream meant.
ISHMAEL: Maybe it didn't mean anything.
EMILIE: Dreams can't not mean anything.
ISHMAEL: Sure they can. Sometimes I have weird dreams 'cause I eat right before I go to bed — I have a dream, and all it means was that I shouldn't have had that steak-umms sandwich.
EMILIE: This wasn't that kind of dream.
ISHMAEL: *(Sighing.)* You're going to tell me now, aren't you.
EMILIE: There was this sound — I thought it was an appliance or a helicopter, something, at first, but then I realized — it was birds' wings. Hundreds and hundreds of birds' wings —
    (The sound starts again, softly).
    — and then I realized that they were gathered here. All around the edge

of the bed. They were all kinds of sizes — big, small, mother, chick, and they were all different types of colors. Blue, red —

ISHMAEL: Green. Or a sort of green-brown, like khaki —

(The sound stops).

EMILIE: Yes! You've had it too?

ISHMAEL: Last week — I was wondering what happened to that dream.

(He turns back over to go to sleep).

EMILIE: Wait a minute — are you saying —

ISHMAEL: I had that dream last week.

EMILIE: But —

ISHMAEL: But I haven't been having it lately. I guess you took it.

EMILIE: Excuse me? Are you calling me some kind of . . . dream stealer?

ISHMAEL: Emilie . . .

EMILIE: I am not a dream stealer! I am perfectly capable of having my own dreams.

ISHMAEL: Of course you are.

EMILIE: So then —

ISHMAEL: All I know is that last week I was having it, and now you're having it. It must have passed to you, somehow.

EMILIE: So what does it mean?

ISHMAEL: I don't know. Some couples start to look like each other, after a while. Heh. Maybe some couples start having each others' dreams.

(Pause.)

EMILIE: What are you dreaming about?

ISHMAEL: Nothing too interesting.

EMILIE: But what?

ISHMAEL: Emilie . . . can't we discuss this in the morning?

EMILIE: Just tell me what you were dreaming about.

ISHMAEL: Why?

EMILIE: I had your dream — maybe you had mine.

ISHMAEL: I don't think so.

EMILIE: Why not?

ISHMAEL: I think I'd know if I had a woman's dream.

EMILIE: You are such a . . .

(She pauses, guessing)

You know — women can dream about power tools too.

(Ishmael sits up).

ISHMAEL: What?

EMILIE: You *are* having my dream, aren't you?

ISHMAEL: You mean you used to dream about taking a chain saw and —

EMILIE: — cutting the huge branch off the tree that used to make that horrible scraping noise against the window? Yep.

ISHMAEL: Huh.

EMILIE: What?

ISHMAEL: I wouldn't have figured you for such a . . .

EMILIE: Such a . . .

ISHMAEL: *Mundane* dreamer.

EMILIE: *Mundane?*

ISHMAEL: OK, bad word choice. I just always figured you must have pretty fan-
tastical dreams.

EMILIE: And now?

ISHMAEL: Now . . . nothing.

EMILIE: You think less of me, don't you?

ISHMAEL: No . . .

EMILIE: You thought my dreams were all exciting and spectacular and mysterious, and now —

ISHMAEL: Now *nothing.* Just forget about it.
    (Pause.)

EMILIE: Your dream is scary.

ISHMAEL: Mmmm?

EMILIE: Your dream. Your thousand-birds-beating-their-wings-fast-around-our-
bed-trying-to-lift-our-mattress dream. It's scary.

ISHMAEL: They're lifting the mattress?

EMILIE: Oh yeah.
    (Pause.)

EMILIE: Where did that dream come from?

ISHMAEL: I don't know. I figure I must've caught a few minutes of *The Birds*
when I was channel-surfing.

EMILIE: Oh, don't tell me that.

ISHMAEL: What?

EMILIE: I don't want our dream to have come from something on TV.

ISHMAEL: *Our* dream?

EMILIE: Well, we've both dreamt it now, haven't we?

ISHMAEL: Yeah.

EMILIE: Do you think they're interconnected?

ISHMAEL: What?

EMILIE: Our dreams. Do you think they go together? Like, maybe because I
cut down —

ISHMAEL: *I* cut it down — I had the dream last . . .

EMILIE: Fine — do you think because *we* cut down the tree branch, the birds that lived on it in real life are getting revenge? Like, their spirits are coming after us?

ISHMAEL: Nah — no birds lived on that branch, in real life. They checked it out first, remember?

EMILIE: Oh. Right.

(Pause. She pokes Ishmael.)

Hey — they're not lifting the mattress in your version?

ISHMAEL: Huh?

EMILIE: You said that when you had the dream, the birds weren't lifting the mattress?

ISHMAEL: Nope, they weren't.

EMILIE: So . . . what were they doing?

ISHMAEL: Bird things. Grooming, feeding, nesting . . .

EMILIE: They start out doing that, in my dream.

(The sound of wings beating starts again).

But then, they all stop doing bird things and get this really . . . *purposeful* look in their eyes.

(The sound gets louder).

And they all grab bits of the mattress in their beaks, and they flap, and . . . we start to rise.

ISHMAEL: Wow — those are some strong birds.

(The sound stops).

EMILIE: Wait a minute — I don't remember seeing you.

ISHMAEL: Huh?

EMILIE: In the dream — when the mattress starts to rise, I turn to say something to you, and you're not there. What does it mean? Why are they trying to fly off with *me?*

ISHMAEL: I told you, I don't *know.*

(He turns over.)

EMILIE: Why aren't you curious?

ISHMAEL: Because I'm tired! Because I don't believe in dreams, because . . . I don't know, I just don't care.

(Pause.)

EMILIE: You don't care that I can't go to sleep?

ISHMAEL: Try drinking some warm milk — or a couple of bites of turkey — tryptophan, you know —

EMILIE: No, I don't mean that I *can't* sleep, I mean that I don't *want* to. I'm scared to.

ISHMAEL: Why?

EMILIE: Hello! What have we been talking about this whole time — the dream — your fucking scary, monster-multicolored-bird dream! I can't sleep now, and it's all your fault!

ISHMAEL: Why is it my fault?

EMILIE: Because you gave me your dream!

ISHMAEL: I didn't give it to you — you took it! Besides, what's the big deal — it's just some birds —

EMILIE: They're not just "some birds," these are birds with a purpose, with an *agenda.* They get that look in their eyes — like you when you want to have sex.

ISHMAEL: When it was *my* dream, they didn't act like that. When it was *my* dream, they were perfectly peaceful. You took my dream and made it yours — you're the one who made it scary. Maybe it's what you deserve. *(He gets out of bed and grabs a pillow and a blanket).*

EMILIE: What are you talking about?

ISHMAEL: You always want to share everything — thoughts, feelings, entrees. You take my dream, make it into something scary, and then blame me. Can't I at least have my unconscious to myself? Is it too much to ask to be allowed to keep *some* things to myself?
(He starts to exit.)

EMILIE: Hey! You took *my* dream, you know.

ISHMAEL: Uh-uh. You forced it on me. Your dull, boring, dream — you made me take it.

EMILIE: I did not! And it's not boring!
(Ishmael starts to leave again.)

EMILIE: What are you doing? Where are you going?

ISHMAEL: To the couch — my *own* place to sleep.

EMILIE: But —

ISHMAEL: It's your dream now — you figure it out.

EMILIE: Ishmael! Ishmael! Please don't go . . .
(He exits. Silence. Emilie sits there for a moment.)

EMILIE: OK — no big deal — it's just a dream.
(She sits on the edge of the bed.)
It's just a dream.
(She gets into bed, under the covers.)
It's just . . . *(She yawns.)* a dream.
(As she starts to fall asleep, the sound of beating wings begins again, and grows louder and louder — as the sound reaches its climax, blackout.)

END OF PLAY

SOMETIMES ROMEO IS SAD

SUZANNE BRADBEER

With a shout out to Margarett Perry

Sometimes Romeo Is Sad was read in June 2006 as part of the Lark Underground: a monthly presentation of new work by the Lark Play Development Center, John Clinton Eisner, Artistic Director. With Jennifer Dorr White as Margot and Will Harper as Mike.

CHARACTERS

(*Color-blind casting is encouraged.*)

MARGOT, forty-ish. An actress. Very talented, very underappreciated: Life Is Not Fair.

MIKE, twenties. Wouldn't look out of place on a motorcycle.

TIME AND PLACE

The rehearsal room in a brand new but richly endowed regional theater. First day of rehearsal.

• • •

Lights up on Margot with a sword, practicing combat moves. She is very good and very intent. Mike enters, watches her.

MARGOT: (*Irritated.*) I see you.

MIKE: I see you too.

MARGOT: You shouldn't sneak up like that on a person.

MIKE: You're good. Where'd you learn all that?

MARGOT: In New York.

MIKE: New York, no kidding.

MARGOT: Yeah, no kidding, listen, your class went that way, Mr. Hardy's drama class, right? From the high school? I met all your classmates. Christ, the enthusiasm — it's just a rehearsal room, folks!

MIKE: How about showing me a few moves, with the weaponry?

MARGOT: I don't think so.

MIKE: C'mon.

MARGOT: Look at you: so eager, so young, so . . . ridiculously attractive — can I give you some advice? RUN. If you're entertaining the least idea of pursuing this profession — run the other way, I'm not kidding. OK, enjoy it in high school. Do *Pippin,* or *Streetcar,* or *Jesus Hopped the A Train* for all I care, but then let that be enough, for God's sake, let that be enough.

MIKE: Well I sure appreciate the excellent advice and everything but —

MARGOT: Yeah, I can see it in your eyes — it's like a drug, right? Listen to me — just do drugs! I shouldn't say that — don't do drugs. They'll ruin your life. I've never tried them, but believe me, I know. I mean, I've tried pot, who hasn't, but that doesn't really count. I mean it does count, you haven't tried it have you? It's a scourge, really, I only tried it 'cause I thought I had glaucoma. OK? So don't do drugs. And don't do theater.

It'll break your heart. Really. This is no joke. Now go away. *(She motions with her sword.)*

MIKE: They say it's a great place to meet the ladies.

MARGOT: OK, you know what? You really need to leave now because I kind of feel like injuring people.

MIKE: *Damn.*

MARGOT: Yesterday my boyfriend broke up with me over the phone; broke up with me because his first day on tour he found himself *suddenly* in love with the girl playing Maria. So last night, to pay him back I had a one-night stand with a bounty hunter named Buck, who drinks Coors and looks a lot like Rush Limbaugh. Meaning, if you don't leave soon, I can't be accountable, I really don't think I can be held accountable for any untoward actions that I might take.

MIKE: I think I can handle myself.

MARGOT: Is that a threat, are you threatening me? Because I know people. I know Buck. Buck has a gun.

MIKE: I'm not threatening you –

MARGOT: Handle yourself, what does that mean — no, I know what that means, you think I don't understand code, the code language of "handling yourself"? You pretend to be part of Mr. Hardy's class and I give you really good advice from the heart and then you speak this threatening code language, you think I've never been to the "hood"?

MIKE: Lady, what is your problem? Ease up.

MARGOT: . . . I can't!

MIKE: Look, this is my philosophy, do you want to hear my philosophy?

MARGOT: No.

MIKE: The sun rises, the sky is blue, the toilet flushes, this is good.

MARGOT: That's not a *philosophy.*

MIKE: The shower works, this is good; the cigarette is good, the Coca-Cola, the Pop-Tart, the second cigarette, all good. The Broncos won last night, very good. I have refrained from dropping by Crazy Al's for the last thirty-one days in a row: very, very good. Today I get to go to rehearsal, good, good, great. Oh shit, I'm an hour early to rehearsal, must have got the time wrong, this is not *as* good, but it's not bad either. *(Referring to Margot.)* I see a vision, this is good, the vision's got a sword, this is better. And then the vision speaks. Not so good.

MARGOT: Vision? You think I'm a, vision?

MIKE: A lovely vision, all in black. I'm Mike. Mike Stevens.

MARGOT: You're in the cast.

MIKE: That's right.

MARGOT: You're Romeo.

MIKE: My name, dear saint, is hateful to myself.

MARGOT: You're kind of old for Romeo.

MIKE: You thought I was in high school.

MARGOT: Yeah, well, now I'm noticing that you're not. I'm Margot.

MIKE: Hey, how's it going — I mean — not so well I guess, that's too bad.

MARGOT: I'm sorry about all the — great first impression, God, could this day get any worse? I'm not crazy OK, I just thought I'd get here early to work off a little of Buck's bad vibe — I hate this play, can I just say that? Romeo and Juliet, I hate you both and I hate your stupid play. I'm glad you die, you couldn't have died soon enough for my taste, and I hope it was very painful.

MIKE: They die?

MARGOT: What?

MIKE: But the love, the love . . .

MARGOT: What love? They hardly knew each other. Can that be love? I don't think so. People do not fall in love at first sight and I, for one, am never doing that again.

MIKE: That's quite a philosophy, Lady —

(Mike walks over to Margot, she instinctively backs up.)

MARGOT: It's not a philo — what're you doing?!

(He moves a little closer.)

MIKE: Where'd you get this? Or did you just bring your own?

(Mike takes the blade from Margot. He's standing too close.)

MARGOT: I got it over there.

(She motions to the side of the room. He doesn't move.)

In the cabinet.

(He still hasn't moved.)

Which is over there.

(He still hasn't moved.)

Please stop staring at me.

(He still hasn't moved nor stopped staring.)

MIKE: I saw you in the other play.

MARGOT: What?

MIKE: You were really good.

MARGOT: OK . . .

MIKE: I mean, really good.

MARGOT: . . . Thanks.

MIKE: I saw it seventeen times.

MARGOT: Seventeen times? You saw me seventeen times? That's a little disturbing. And, flattering! I'm actually very flattered, seventeen times to see me, that's so —

MIKE: This girl I knew was in it, you probably know her.

MARGOT: What girl?

MIKE: Colette.

MARGOT: Colette? Of the tits?

MIKE: That's her.

MARGOT: She's your girl, your girlfriend?

MIKE: Girlfriend, I don't know, that's kind of a strong word.

MARGOT: Yeah, OK, I get it. She's an interesting person, Colette. Is she still doing that dancing? What do you call it?

MIKE: Pole dancing. She says "hi."

MARGOT: Seventeen times. Seventeen times. And to see Colette, wow, some people might find that a little — and yet, *girlfriend* is kind of a strong word for you? Men. I've had it. I've really just about had it.

MIKE: Is there a special way to hold this thing?

MARGOT: Fickle, faithless fucks. There. I said it. (*She grabs her sword back and threatens him with it.*)

MIKE: Careful, I don't know how to defend myself yet.

MARGOT: Fucks, fucks, fucks!! Assholes!!!

MIKE: I didn't see it that many times for Colette —

MARGOT: Asshole fucks — what?

MIKE: Colette's not my girlfriend. She's a nice girl I saw a couple of times.

MARGOT: Seventeen times! That's called obsession!

MIKE: You try spending six years on the inside, you might get a little obsessed about some things too.

MARGOT: On the "inside"?

MIKE: Shit.

MARGOT: The inside of what?

MIKE: Nothing. Well, OK. Prison.

MARGOT: Prison? You're a, a, a con?

MIKE: Ex-con.

MARGOT: OK, back off, buddy.

MIKE: (*This really matters to him.*) No, no, see — while I was in prison I had a lot of time to think about things. About what is important and I developed this philosophy —

MARGOT: Yeah I remember your life-is-a-bowl-of-cherries philosophy —

MIKE: No, this one is about love –

MARGOT: Listen, I think I should go somewhere else for awhile, Mike. Until rehearsal starts.

MIKE: Why? Are you worried about the prison thing? It was just marijuana. It was A LOT of marijuana, but –

MARGOT: It's not the prison thing.

MIKE: Then what?

(She moves to the door.)

MARGOT: Cause you're so happy to be here, and you believe in love, and you should. But I'm not happy, and I don't believe, and I don't want to affect your glowy happy enthusiasm — it's obnoxious. I mean, you're also happy that the toilet flushes and the shower works. And OK it's not obnoxious, it's beautiful. I wish that stuff made me happy, and maybe it did once, I can't remember anymore, but now everything just makes me mad — I'm just a miserable, old, mean-spirited angry person and I just think I should be all that by myself.

(She starts to walk out.)

MIKE: I can't believe I've already alienated my Juliet.

MARGOT: Your who, what do you mean, I'm not your Juliet.

MIKE: You're not? I'd been thinking of you as Juliet.

MARGOT: Me? Really? Me? You thought I — you know you're right, why not, there's a grand tradition, Peggy Ashcroft, wasn't she, and I'm sure there have been many older, it's a terrific part, but you do need a certain understanding, of course the Nurse is a great part too, I'm not complaining . . . *(At Mike's blank look.)* . . . did you even read the play?

MIKE: I read a scene. And a speech.

MARGOT: A scene and a — how did you get the part?

MIKE: I read a scene and a speech. For the guy.

MARGOT: The guy? You mean, the director?

MIKE: That's him.

MARGOT: Have you ever done a play before? Any play?

MIKE: I've seen a couple. Mostly a lot of TV though. Especially these last six years or so.

MARGOT: And they're having you play the lead, in Shakespeare? Oh my God. You're one of those people aren't you? One of those good-looking ex-con people that gets told, "Oh, you're so good-looking, you should be an actor." But even good-looking ex-con people read the damn play, Bub. Where is everybody? Isn't it time for the rest of these people to start arriving? Where's the stage manager, what time is it? *(She looks at him.)* Are you, are you *crying?*

MIKE: Everyone said it would be hard acclimating —

MARGOT: Oh, oh no, oh no no no. Don't listen to me, that's probably the first thing you should know about me. Hey — it's fine that you're good-looking, there's nothing wrong with being good-looking or an ex-con. You're going to be great and good-looking in this part, I'm sure.

MIKE: I've never been on a stage, I've never even read a whole play, this is so pitiful.

MARGOT: What is the most important quality of Romeo? That he be attractive, right? You're very attractive. Don't cry.

MIKE: I don't even know how to hold a sword!

MARGOT: Look, here, look, I'll show you. (*She walks over, placing his hand correctly on the handle.*) Put your thumb there, that's right. And your fingers . . . like this. Hold the handle with confidence, but loose, see? That's right, that's right, you're doing great. Now your shoulders . . . do you mind if I . . . (*She adjusts his shoulders.*) See, you're a natural, you're really a . . . you know, you have very good arms for this kind of thing, they're excellent, excellent arms that you have . . . (*They are standing very close.*)

MIKE: So what's the idea, is there a philosophy behind this kind of combat?

MARGOT: I guess the, philosophy, is to get one's adversary without being, gotten.

MIKE: I don't believe in that philosophy.

MARGOT: You should. It's terribly important, a terribly, terribly important philosophy . . .

(*The sword clatters to the floor, and Mike and Margot are kissing, passionately. They break apart*).

MARGOT: (*Continued.*) Oh, help.

END OF PLAY

SUPERHERO

MARK HARVEY LEVINE

Superhero was first produced by ZJU Theatre Group (Los Angeles, California) in June 2002. It was directed by Mark Harvey Levine, with the following cast: Rachel — Joan Giammarco; Leonard — Cary Dean Bazan. *Superhero* had its first Equity production as part of *Cabfare For The Common Man* at The Phoenix Theatre (Indianapolis, Indiana) in May 2005. Bryan D. Fonseca was the artistic director. It was directed by Bryan D. Fonseca, with the following cast: Rachel — Deborah Sargent; Leonard — Jon Lindley.

CHARACTERS
RACHEL, twenties to thirties, a little agoraphobic
LEONARD, slight, twenties to thirties, believes himself to be a superhero.

SETTING
Rachel's one-bedroom apartment. It contains a small table with several chairs and lots of clutter.

• • •

An apartment; morning. At lights up, Rachel is seen bound to a chair, a gag in her mouth.

RACHEL: *(Muffled from the gag.)* Help . . . help!
  (There is a loud thump, the sound of somebody running into the door.)
RACHEL: *(Continued.)* Oh, wait, it's locked.
  (Rachel effortlessly gets out of the chair, unlocks her front door, and returns to the chair, "re-tying" herself.)
RACHEL: *(Continued.)* Try it again. *(She puts the gag back on her mouth.)*
  (Nothing happens.)
RACHEL: *(Continued.) (Sighing.)* Help, help.
  (Immediately, Leonard bursts through her door. He is a slight man dressed like a superhero. His costume is obviously, and rather pathetically, homemade.)
LEONARD: *(His slogan.)* I'm here to help!
RACHEL: Thank God you're here.
LEONARD: I picked up your cry for help. Luckily, I was in the hallway taking out my garbage at the time. What happened, citizen?
RACHEL: Ruffians!
LEONARD: *(He starts to untie her, not noticing how easy it is.)* Ruffians?
RACHEL: They tried to rob me. But they heard you and ran.
LEONARD: They won't get far. *(His exit line.)* Stay strong, citizen!
  (He starts to leave.)
RACHEL: Leonard! Don't go!—
LEONARD: I'm not Leonard! Leonard is my friend. He helps me in my exploits.
RACHEL: Oh, sorry, sorry. I forgot. But I have to call you something — you haven't picked out your name yet.
LEONARD: My name has to come from my powers. And I don't know what they are — yet. I know I can't fly. *(Obviously there's a story here.)*
RACHEL: You'll figure it out.
LEONARD: *(Preparing to leave again.)* Stay strong, citizen.

RACHEL: Wait! Help!

LEONARD: What's wrong?

RACHEL: Well, it's just . . . um . . . *(Indicates pastry box nearby.)* I've got all these danishes, and I won't be able to eat 'em all. Want one?

(She pulls out a chair for him.)

LEONARD: That's not a—! You— It's—

(He's frustrated into speechlessness.)

RACHEL: If you don't eat it, it'll go to waste! Isn't it a crime to waste food?!

LEONARD: Yes, but —

RACHEL: Well, here is a crime you can prevent! Have some breakfast. You want coffee?

LEONARD: I'm on duty!

RACHEL: Superheroes can't sit down and eat a meal?

LEONARD: At this very moment I'm locked in a terrible struggle with Claw Woman.

RACHEL: Claw Woman?!

LEONARD: . . . You may know her as Esther Manning, in 316.

RACHEL: Oh yeah! Her. With all the cats.

LEONARD: She's a Grasping Harpy of Evil. Our contest of wills has escalated. Only one of us will survive.

RACHEL: Well, you can't defeat her on an empty stomach. Have you eaten anything yet?

LEONARD: . . . I had a bowl of frosted flakes.

RACHEL: You're running around on nothing but cereal?! Now that is a crime. Sit down. I've got apricot.

LEONARD: Apricot . . . My favorite. Resistance . . . weakening . . . Getting . . . hungry . . . Must . . . turn . . . away . . .

RACHEL: Want me to heat 'em up?

LEONARD: No! What if evil strikes and I'm sitting here with a mouth full of tangy apricot filling? I have to go. Stay strong!

(He goes to leave again.)

RACHEL: Oh wait, help! Sorry, sorry, there's one more thing. If you don't mind.

LEONARD: Now what?

RACHEL: Well . . .

LEONARD: Your life had better be in danger.

RACHEL: Well . . . um, I can't get to that bulb up there.

LEONARD: You want me . . . to change a lightbulb?!

RACHEL: I thought with your super-height, you could reach it. Sorry.

LEONARD: Rachel, you've got to stop calling me in, unless it's an actual emergency! I'm a superhero!

RACHEL: I know. I'm sorry.

LEONARD: What if someone's really in trouble, and I'm here . . . fixing your disposal?!

RACHEL: Sorry, sorry.

LEONARD: . . . How IS the disposal, by the way?

RACHEL: Oh, it's great! You did a fabulous job with —

LEONARD: All right then. 'Sides, you don't need a superhero, you need the super. Where IS Mr. Crazciek?

RACHEL: He won't come up to this floor since you defeated him in battle.

LEONARD: Right. Now, Rachel. I'm going to change your lightbulb, as a favor, because you're a nice person.

(He gets a chair and stands on it.)

LEONARD: *(Continued.)* But then you must never call me again, unless it's an actual life-or-death emergency. Not to change a lightbulb, not to set your VCR, not to buy you the paper. This is it.

RACHEL: *(Unreasonably worried about him on the chair.)* Ooo, careful . . .

LEONARD: I don't run errands — I fight evil!

RACHEL: *(The old schoolyard trick, she grabs him and shakes him.)* Saved your life! *(She laughs a little too giddily, stays hanging on.)*

LEONARD: Rachel . . . you wanna let me go?

RACHEL: *(Reluctantly lets go of him, overly nervous.)* OK! I'm sorry. Please be careful. Please.

LEONARD: This is nothing! I spent all yesterday battling Claw Woman and her Cat Minions. Get me a new bulb.

RACHEL: *(As she does so.)* How many cats DOES she have?!

LEONARD: I think she has all of them.

RACHEL: *(Finding the bulb, unreasonably scared for Leonard.)* Yeah, seriously . . . Ooo! Careful! Careful!

LEONARD: *(She hands him the bulb.)* They keep getting on my balcony and attacking my plants. They killed my ficus. I must avenge his death. *(Like a comic book:)* The bulb! I— I can't reach it!

RACHEL: That's OK, that's OK, just get down, get down!

LEONARD: You think I accept defeat so easily? Ha!

(He stacks two or three chairs on top of one another. It looks incredibly precarious. He starts to climb up.)

RACHEL: *(Completely panicked.)* NO! DON'T! *(She restrains him.)*

LEONARD: What? What's the matter with you?

RACHEL: You're going to get hurt! Don't!

LEONARD: Rachel, please!

RACHEL: No! No! You're going to fall and break your neck and it'll be my fault! Please! Forget the light! Please!

LEONARD: All right, all right . . . calm down! Sheesh!

RACHEL: I'm sorry. It's just — I'm afraid of heights.

LEONARD: You were on the ground.

RACHEL: I'm afraid of heights for other people.

LEONARD: You weren't in danger, Rachel.

RACHEL: I am in danger! We all are! Look at this! *(She grabs the newspaper.)* Bus crashes, home-invasion murders, random shootings, breast cancer, bridge collapses, killer bees! Ewgh! *(She rips an article out of the paper.)* I am in danger! I'm in terrible danger, Leonard!

LEONARD: *(Angrily.)* I'm not Leonard! Leonard is, like you, afraid of everything! Leonard goes to work alone and comes home alone and sits alone in his apartment and eats his meals over the sink and watches TV until he falls asleep. But not me.

RACHEL: OK —

LEONARD: That's how I found out I was a superhero. I always WAS one, but I didn't know it! Nobody told me! They kept it hidden from me!

RACHEL: OK, OK, shh, shh, relax honey.

LEONARD: *(Getting very worked up.)* I should have known, though. It was there all the time. How come I always got the parking ticket, the broken shoelace? How come I always arrive JUST as they're flipping over the sign that says "closed"? Why do they imitate my voice at work when they think I'm not around? Why such a large conspiracy to destroy me? There can only be one reason! I'm dangerous to them!

RACHEL: *(Afraid.)* Yes, you are, honey, you are, you are.

LEONARD: Now, I don't know what my powers are, but I do know that I'm brave! Strong! Invincible!

RACHEL: That's very —

LEONARD: *(Coming at her.)* I'm afraid of nothing!

RACHEL: *(Backing into a corner.)* I'm a little afraid of you, I'm afraid.

LEONARD: You're afraid of everything! Just like Leonard —

RACHEL: It's true, it's true! I'm a chicken! I'm afraid of bugs, and microwave ovens, and cancer and subways and Rod Stewart and nuclear war —

LEONARD: They did this to you, Rachel! Don't you see? It's just what happened to Leonard. When you were in school, were you the last person picked for the team?

RACHEL: Always.

LEONARD: When you stand at the deli, does the lady behind the counter stare into space like you're not even there?

RACHEL: Yes . . .

LEONARD: Have you been ignored, insulted, discarded all your life?

RACHEL: Yes!

LEONARD: Rachel! You're a superhero!

RACHEL: *(Laughs nervously.)* Oh no no no.

LEONARD: You are, and you don't know it!

RACHEL: Oh, no. Please. Are you kidding me? I'm nobody.

LEONARD: That's what I thought. But you'll know when you put the uniform on. Try it.

RACHEL: Oh, no, no, that's all right, really —

LEONARD: I'm serious. *(As in a comic book.)* You have no idea the power you'll feel — pure energy coursing through your veins! *(Then, as himself.)* It's really kinda cool!

RACHEL: No, thanks.

LEONARD: Come on.

RACHEL: . . . Well, maybe just the cape.

(He removes his cape and puts it on her.)

LEONARD: There. How do you feel?

RACHEL: Like a lady in a cape.

LEONARD: You have to have the gloves, too.

(He removes his gloves, she puts them on. During this —)

LEONARD: They go with the cape.

RACHEL: And very smartly, too.

(He hands her the underwear.)

RACHEL: Um . . .

LEONARD: I've only worn these on the outside.

RACHEL: Sorry, I had to ask.

(She puts them over her slacks.)

LEONARD: OK . . . now . . . the mask.

RACHEL: Is that OK?

LEONARD: I . . . I guess so. I mean, if you want to get the whole effect . . .

(Leonard removes his mask. Rachel smiles at him. Leonard looks expectantly, and she realizes what she's supposed to do.)

RACHEL: My God! Leonard! It's you!

LEONARD: Yes . . . It's me. I had to conceal my identity from you, for your own safety. But now . . . well, there are no secrets between superheroes.

RACHEL: Oh, honey . . . I'm not a superhero.

LEONARD: Aren't you? Put on the mask.

(She does. She now has Leonard's costume on, and he is more or less normally dressed.)

LEONARD: *(Continued.)* You sure look like one. Try walking around.
    (She shuffles around.)

LEONARD: *(Continued.)* No, no! You have to stride forward, with purpose! Fists clenched! Head high! Never turn back! You turn back, you trip over your cape. How do you feel?

RACHEL: Completely ridiculous. Leonard, I don't think I'm cut out to be a superhero . . .

LEONARD: Of course you are . . . I can't be wrong about this. I'm never wrong about this.

RACHEL: Leonard, I'm just the lady who lives across the hall from you. If you want, you can come over and have breakfast sometim —

LEONARD: Fine then! Have it your way! And you can spend the rest of your life getting the parking tickets, the leaky faucets, and the dead plants! Because you're a loser! A failure! You SHOULD be picked last for the team! You should be laughed at and passed over and ignored and —
    (Quite suddenly, Rachel slugs him in the jaw, surprising herself as well as Leonard. He goes down hard.)

RACHEL: OhmiGod!

LEONARD: *(From the floor.)* . . . Nicely done . . .

RACHEL: OhmiGod! Are you OK?! I'm so sorry! I don't know why I did that! Are you OK?

LEONARD: *(In great pain.)* Sure . . . No problem . . . Don't forget, I'm a superhero. And so are you. Feels good, huh?

RACHEL: I've never hit anyone before!

LEONARD: Well you're . . . doing swell, for a beginner.

RACHEL: I can't believe I —

LEONARD: It's the uniform. It's amazing what it does, isn't it?

RACHEL: Yeah, I guess so . . .

LEONARD: Congratulations. Today, for the first time, you fought back against the forces of evil!

RACHEL: I did?

LEONARD: Sure. That nasty little voice inside you? I've got one, too. Of course, I also have Claw Woman in 316.
    (She laughs.)

RACHEL: Leonard, I think you've . . . awakened my inner Wonder Woman . . .
    (She climbs up on the chair. She poses, superhero-lly.)

RACHEL: *(Continued.)* Hey.

LEONARD: What?

RACHEL: Hey!

LEONARD: What?!
RACHEL: You saved my life . . .
   (Lights fade.)

END OF PLAY

PLAYS FOR
TWO MEN

BE THE HUNTER

Tom Coash

CHARACTERS

BOBBY, male, between eighteen and twenty-one years old, a Marine, dressed in shorts, tennis shoes with no socks, and a colorful Hawaiian shirt. Smart and a smart-ass.

QUINT, male, eighteen to twenty-one years old, known Bobby since childhood, dressed from head to toe in hunting/camouflage gear, boots, shades. A good old boy.

SETTING

The woods, mid-morning

TIME

The present

. . .

Bright fall day. A clearing in the woods. Bobby, dressed in jeans and Hawaiian shirt, sits on a log, rifle next to him, smoking a cigarette and drinking vodka out of a quart bottle. We hear sporadic gunshots in the distance. Quint, rifle in hand, shades, dressed from head to toe in camouflage gear, rises from behind a rock and creeps up behind Bobby and raises the gun to his head.

QUINT: You're dead raghead!

BOBBY: Hoo-aah.

QUINT: Down on the ground dickweed. 'Fore I waste you!

BOBBY: You're forgetting something.

QUINT: What?

BOBBY: Hearts and minds, dude.

QUINT: What?

BOBBY: You're sposed to win our hearts and minds. For freedom and democracy.

QUINT: How do I waste your ass and win your heart and mind at the same-time?

BOBBY: "Operation Freedom," man. Not "Operation Waste Their Asses."
(Offers Quint the flask, who waves it off.)

QUINT: Come on, get up. I wanta shoot something.
(Swings his rifle around the clearing.)
Boom! Boom! Boom!

BOBBY: Nice.

QUINT: We're sposed to be huntin', not sitting here rotatin'.

BOBBY: Like there's deer round here after that.

QUINT: Like there's deer round here at three in the afternoon. What happened to "get out at the crack o' dawn"?

BOBBY: Sounds like somebody's shooting at something.

QUINT: Shit, buncha drunks haulin' around in their Ass UVs killing cows. You wanna hunt deer, you build a stand, you wear camo, you're here at dawn, you're serious about it. This is bullshit. Three in the fuckin' PM. You used to be serious about this. Fucking DeerHunter, man. I used to look up to you.

BOBBY: Hoo-aahh.

QUINT: Fuckin' Daniel Boone.

BOBBY: Shit.

QUINT: Fuckin' Euell Gibbons with a hard-on. Living off the land!

BOBBY: Be the hunter.

QUINT: Fuckin' A, Bro.

BOBBY: That's what our Division Commander told us. Before we went in to Falluja.

QUINT: What?

BOBBY: Be the hunter.

QUINT: No shit?

BOBBY: You should hear this asshole. Feeding us all this garbage about how we were following in the footsteps of Alexander the Great. Like the fucking Hoplites.

QUINT: *(Making machine-gun sounds . . .)* Buuurrrooowww, .50 caliber, buur-rrooww! Run you fuckin' hadjis!

BOBBY: Can you believe that shit?

QUINT: "Be the hunter"! I like that. *(Pause.)* So I was pretty good, hunh?

BOBBY: What?

QUINT: Snuck up on your ass cold.

BOBBY: You were dead ten times over.

QUINT: No way. *(Bobby shrugs.)* No way you saw me.

BOBBY: RAP round right up your ass.

QUINT: Good cover all the way. Your ass was grass. *(Bobby smiles.)* What? I was like Rambo. Navy Seal. Slit your throat, you never hear a thing.

BOBBY: You were behind the trees?

QUINT: I was a tree. A fucking oak, man. Dappled.

BOBBY: There're no trees over there.

QUINT: What?

BOBBY: It's desert. No trees.

QUINT: Oh for Christ sake.

BOBBY: You're lying there in the dirt, gutshot, intestines spewing all over your lap.

QUINT: Right.

BOBBY: Lying there screaming. Sand in your eyes. Flies on your face.

QUINT: Palm trees.

BOBBY: No.

QUINT: Coconut trees.

BOBBY: There's no trees!! They all got wasted! Burned, blasted! It's a goddamn desert! All right?!!

QUINT: All right.

BOBBY: There's no trees!

QUINT: OK, OK.

BOBBY: I oughta know! I fucking know!

QUINT: OK, Jesus. Chill! *(Pause.)* You're wack sometimes, man. You known-that?

BOBBY: *(Bobby chugs the rest of the bottle and tosses it.)* You ever wish you were a girl?

QUINT: A girl?

BOBBY: Women in the service get pregnant, they stay home.

QUINT: Uh oh, Branson got some barracks babe prego?

BOBBY: I'm not going back, man.

QUINT: Some sweet little barracks Ho?

BOBBY: It's too fucked up.

QUINT: What? You and some chick?

BOBBY: The war, dipstick. If I was a woman, I could conveniently forget my fucking pill, get knocked up, and nobody'd care.

QUINT: Whoa, whoa, whoa, back up some.

BOBBY: And you're gonna help me.

QUINT: I'm gonna get you pregnant?

BOBBY: You're gonna shoot me.

QUINT: Shoot you?!

BOBBY: You shoot me in the leg, I don't have to go back.

QUINT: The hell you don't have to go back.

BOBBY: An unfortunate hunting accident.

QUINT: They'd throw your ass in the slammer.

BOBBY: Happens every year. Poor fucker gets mistaken for Bambi. Blammo.

QUINT: You're saying you want to go AWOL?

BOBBY: I'm saying I don't believe in what we're doing over there and I don't wanta fucking die for it. Simple.

QUINT: Simple?

BOBBY: *(Cocks a finger at his leg.)* Bam! I'm home free. Million-dollar wound.

QUINT: Shit. *(Pause.)* Mr. Gung-Ho Marine! Mr. Fuckin' Devil Dog, Green Dragon gonna whip their Arab asses.

BOBBY: You don't know what you're talking about, man.

QUINT: You're on a mission! That's what you said! That you were on a mission to spread the gospel of America and the M-16.

BOBBY: Fucking recruiter fed me that bullshit. And you know what? We were! We were on a mission. Now we're just standing around with our dicks in our hands waiting for someone to chop 'em off.

QUINT: So all your big talk . . .

BOBBY: Listen, we're s'posed to be freeing these people, right? 'Stead we're just wrecking the goddamn place. The U.S. Wrecking Ball Corp. The old guys say it's like Vietnam all over. No mission. Take ground and give it back. Take Falluja, give it back, take Tikrit, give it back. Nobody wants us there. You think every car on the street an IED packed with nails and dynamite.

QUINT: Shit.

BOBBY: We're manning a roadblock and this beat-up fuckin' Mercedes comes screaming the wrong way up the street at us. Hitting potholes, trunk lid bouncing up and down, horn blaring. We're shooting in the air, shouting, waving it off. Suicide bomber, suicide bomber! People scattering. Upgunner on the LAV lets go with the .50 caliber and that car just disintegrates. Contents? One old fat guy in a scungy galabeya with half a head left. Two dead women in the back. Blood everywhere. Clothes shredded, brains and body parts all over the fucking upholstery. Two little girls and their fucking dolls cut to pieces in the trunk, and then this baby on the floor of the backseat screaming his lungs out. Civilians. They see a Huey overhead and a fucking M1A1 Abrams tank coming down their street and they just panicked. Freaked. God knows what. I'm standin' there like an idiot wiping the mother's brains off this baby's face, yelling for the medevac and suddenly an RPG comes whizzing past me, bounces off the tank and blows sky high. Three of our crew down. AK-47 rounds snappin' all around us. Tracers. There's a goddamn sniper! The tank lets go with the main gun. You could actually see the blast wave going down the street. Blows this building a new fucking double-wide garage door, no more sniper. The LT's yelling something but I can't hear shit. I feel this warm, wet stuff on my chest and look down thinking, fuck I'm hit! Kid's peeing on me. Street's total screaming chaos, bodies everywhere, and his little dick's waving back and forth in the air like a little firehose squirting piss all over me.

QUINT: Jesus.

BOBBY: This is being the hunter?!

QUINT: It's war dude! It's being a soldier.

BOBBY: What war? Not my war. Not their war. We haven't even declared fucking war! We're just sitting ducks minding the pond while these oil assholes are pumping billions out from underneath us.

QUINT: Bullshit, you know it's more than that.

BOBBY: Is it?

QUINT: We're making America safer.

BOBBY: Thank you Mr. President.

QUINT: Making the world safer.

BOBBY: Jesus that shit sounds corny when you say it out loud.

QUINT: It's not corny!

BOBBY: Right, mission accomplished. Storm troopers for world peace. Every night kicking down doors for democracy, women and children wailing and screaming. Nobody speaks English. No furniture, no toilets, no running water, no food, no lights. "Down, down, down!" Shouting "Shut the fuck up!" Trying to cuff somebody's shonky old father in his raggedy-ass underwear. Thinking some fifteen-year-old's gonna come screaming outta the back room with an AK-47, blow your nuts off! Hearts and minds dude, hearts and minds.

QUINT: Go to Canada then. Be a conscientious, chicken-ass, objector!

BOBBY: I'm not a conscientious objector. I just object to whatever the fuck it is we think we're doing there.

(Picks up Quint's rifle and shoves it at him.)

QUINT: No.

BOBBY: You said you wanted to shoot something.

QUINT: Shoot your own fuckin' self!

BOBBY: Can't do it. Powder burns. They'll court martial me for a self-inflicted wound.

QUINT: I can't believe this!

BOBBY: You don't know what it's like.

QUINT: No, but I'm going to.

BOBBY: Oh yeah? How's that?

QUINT: I enlisted.

BOBBY: You what?

QUINT: Volunteered for 29 Palms.

BOBBY: Desert training.

QUINT: Yep.

BOBBY: You dumb fuck.

QUINT: Don't call me that.

BOBBY: Haven't you been listening to me?!

QUINT: Hell yeah, I've been listening to you. All this last year. Spit and polish Branson, the Marine's Marine.

BOBBY: Get out of it.

QUINT: I don't want to get out of it. I'll do my duty and I won't come home cryin' about it.

BOBBY: This is classic.

QUINT: We'll have each other's backs, man. Kick some ass. See the world.

BOBBY: You wanta get my back? Then get it now. Shoot me.

QUINT: No way.

BOBBY: Come on, be the hunter!

QUINT: Jesus, you got medals, the silver star! You're a hero. You can't just throw that shit away. They tied yellow ribbons on every tree in this town when you came back. I had to drive over to Wal-Mart in Dempsey and buy their whole fuckin' stock.

BOBBY: I'm sorry! OK?! I'm sorry I'm not the action figure of your fucking dreams! OK?! NOW TAKE THE GUN! TAKE IT! TAKE IT!
(He shoves the gun in Quint's hands and then marches off about 20 feet. Points to his leg.)
Right here.

QUINT: No!

BOBBY: Watch my knee. I don't wanna be Johnny comes gimping home.

QUINT: I ain't gonna do it Bobby.

BOBBY: *(Pause.)* Jennie wants you to do it.

QUINT: What's she got to do with it?

BOBBY: We're getting married.

QUINT: No. Since when?

BOBBY: She's knocked up.

QUINT: You knocked up my sister.

BOBBY: You don't want her to be a war widow, do you buddy?

QUINT: You knocked up my little sister.

BOBBY: I want to hold a baby again, Quint. Just not in the middle of a fire-fight. I want a family. I want a wife. I want a baby.

QUINT: You fuckin' asshole.

BOBBY: So shoot me.

QUINT: You yellow fuckin' bastard.

BOBBY: Just do it before the vodka wears off.
(Quint raises gun and aims at Bobby's head.)
The leg dickweed!

(Pause . . . lowers aim . . . he purposely fires under Bobby's feet, Bobby jumps, fires again, Bobby jumps, laughs.)
Gotta shoot better then that in Baghdad, old buddy!
(Quint fires, Bobby crumples, grabbing his calf, blood spurts out.)
Shit, shit, shit, shit, shit!!! Uunnnhhh, Jesus!
QUINT: I used to look up to you, man.
(Blackout.)

END OF PLAY

THE BOX

DAN AIBEL

The Box was produced by Flashpoint Theatre Company at Mum Puppettheatre in Philadelphia, as part of the SPARK Festival of ten-minute plays. It ran from July 18 through July23, 2006. The play was directed by Erin Lucas. The roles of A and B were played by Kurt Runco and David Stanger, respectively.

CHARACTERS
A
B

SETTING
A room

.   .   .

A and B: An executive and his lackey. A room. A box can be seen.

A: We've come a long way.

B: We have.

A: Hell of a long way.

B: God.

A: Y'know how far we've come? You can buy a nail clipper for seventy-nine cents.

B: Yes.

A: And that's not nothing.

B: It's not.

A: Gives me pause. I'm telling ya. Goose bumps just thinking about it.
    (Pause.)

A: And sex isn't what it used to be.

B: It's not?

A: You think it is? Well it's not. Hell. It's not even close.
    (Pause.)

B: Y'know what I like? Bread.

A: Now you're talking.

B: Good fresh bread. Nothing like it.

A: A thing unto itself.

B: It is.
    (Pause.)

B: And politics . . .

A: Forget about it.

B: I mean . . .

A: Despicable.

B: It is, isn't it?

A: Just the *word* makes me sick.
    (Pause.)

B: How d'you feel about television?

A: Has its place.

B: I think so.

A: Has a role.

B: I like it. I've grown quite fond of it. *(Beat.)* Y'know the one where he goes around stopping murders?

A: Kills me. Absolutely obliterates me, that one.

> *(Pause.)*

B: Where were we?

A: What?

B: The box.

A: Yes. The box. Yes, that's right. I nearly forgot.

B: You didn't forget?

A: No. How could I? I wouldn't. I wouldn't *think* of it. *(Beat.)* So now where is it?

B: That's it.

A: Where?

B: *That.*

A: That's *it?*

B: They condensed it.

A: *Oh.*

B: Condensed and purified it

A: I see.

> *(A retrieves a pair of gloves and puts them on. He moves to pick up the box.)*

B: Don't hold it too close.

A: No.

B: You're holding it too close.

A: Am I?

B: I think you are.

> *(A moves to set the box down.)*

A: Fascinating.

> *(Pause.)*

A: Seen the one where he goes under cover?

B: Under . . . ?

A: As a botanist.

B: A what?

A: A botanist.

B: Oh.

A: You seen it?

B: No.

A: Keep an eye out for it.

B: That right?

A: Keep an eye out for it, that one.

   (Pause.)

B: So.

A: What?

B: *(Referring to the box.)* Well . . . what, um . . . ?

A: Whadda *you* think?

B: Dunno.

A: Tough call, eh?

B: It . . .

A: A rather difficult calculation when you get down to it.

   (Pause.)

A: What about burying?

B: Burying?

A: Wanna bury it?

B: Well . . .

A: Yes?

B: I dunno.

A: We could.

B: Well I dunno, though.

A: What?

B: The groundwater . . .

A: Eh?

B: The groundwater gets involved.

A: It infiltrates the groundwater. Right. Heard about that.

B: Was a PBS special.

A: Was there?

B: Two hours, they did on it.

   (Pause.)

A: Know what I could go for? A smoke.

B: That right?

A: A big fattie fat-fat.

B: Like in the old days.

A: Weren't those the days?

B: My god.

   (Pause.)

A: We could burn it.

B: I was thinking about that.

A: We could up and burn it.

B: And what about . . . ?

A: What?

B: Well, there's talk . . .

A: Yes?

B: There's talk it . . . That it might . . .

A: What?

B: React.

A: React?

B: There's talk.

A: React how?

B: Well it might ignite the atmosphere.

A: No.

B: Well . . .

A: No shit. *(Beat.)* Nix that.

B: Right.

A: Mark down, then, to avoid that.

    (Pause.)

A: Tell me something: What were we thinking? *(Referring to the box.)* Getting involved.

B: *(Referring to the box)* In that?

A: In something so . . .

B: Ages ago, it seems, doesn't it?

A: I mean, what were we, *nuts?*

B: No.

A: Were we *insane?*

B: No.

A: Then what *were* we?

B: Think it was a question of economics.

A: Ah.

B: The economics won out, as I remember.

A: About time.

B: The margins . . .

A: Yes?

B: Very high margins.

A: God, you're right.

B: And the business model . . .

A: It's all coming back to me . . .

B: The business model was . . .

A: Was lean, wasn't it?

B: Quite lean.

A: God it was . . . Never in my life had I seen anything quite that . . . We Had No Inventory!

B: No.

A: How much inventory did we have?

B: None.

A: It was goddamn *brilliant!*

    (Pause.)

A: How about throwing it off a ditch?

B: A cliff?

A: What?

B: A cliff.

A: *(Conceding error.)* Right.

    (Pause.)

A: The one where he doesn't know if he's crazy or they're out to get him?

B: *(Feigning enthusiasm.)* Now that's my favorite.

A: What acting!

B: *(Feigning enthusiasm.)* No, that's my all-time favorite, that one. *(Beat. Worried.)* I just wish it wasn't so contagious.

A: I wish tennis balls weren't so expensive.

B: And toxic.

A: And that smell.

B: So contagious.

A: "Penn number six."

B: Dear God.

A: "Penn number four."

B: They'll string us up.

A: Hypocritical bastards.

    (Pause.)

A: What if we took control of the media?

B: Is that allowed?

A: We'd be nice about it.

B: That permitted, though?

A: Do it by the book. It'd be completely above board.

B: *(Beat.)* Oh: You're talking about a merger.

A: A few *sta*tions . . .

B: I see.

A: . . . couple *channels* . . .

B: We could do that.

A: . . . several *out*lets . . .

B: Could do that, I suppose. *(Beat.)* There would be some hand-wringing.

A: Hand-wringing?

B: And the boys in accounting would have a hell of a time.

A: What hand-wringing?

B: About . . . "corporate journalism."

A: Ah.

B: There'd be criticism.

A: Right.

B: Boycotts.

A: Naturally.

B: An international outcry.

A: I see.

B: For a couple hours, anyway.

> *(Pause.)*

A: And remind me: Why can't we just blame the French?

B: It's passé.

A: Is it?

B: Getting to be passé, I'm afraid.

> *(Pause.)*

B: Y'know what we *could* do: Could pass a law.

A: Won't help.

B: Why not?

A: It Won't Help. It's too late.

B: Don't get moody.

A: Moody?

B: You're getting cranky.

A: *Don't you ever call me cranky!*

> *(Pause.)*

A: What we need is some sort of mass movement.

B: Yes.

A: A groundswell.

B: An uprising of some kind.

A: It's just that they're so lazy.

B: They are.

A: All of them. They're all so damn . . .

B: What if we paid them?

A: *Pay?*

B: If we bribed them.

A: We could incentivize them.

B: With proper incentives, perhaps . . .

A: A . . . a modest stock giveaway.

B: A token equity stake! *(Beat.)* What?

A: Don't like it.

B: But it's perfect!

A: I Don't Like It.

B: But why?

A: *(Beat. Telling a secret.)* The shareholders would shit.

B: *Ah.*

A: Y'know?

B: That's right.

A: Am I right?

B: Forgot all about the "shareholders."

A: *Shh!*

> *(Pause.)*

A: Wait, I got an idea . . .

B: All right.

A: Wait a second . . .

B: What?

A: . . . I've *Got* It: We'll pay your mother-in-law fifty bucks to *hide it in her garage! (Beat.)* Well?

B: Do the words "spontaneous combustion" mean anything to you?

A: Nuts.

B: "Expensive litigation"?

A: You've Made Your Point.

> *(Pause.)*

A: It's not easy.

B: It's not.

A: No easy way out of it. *(Beat.)* The old days? Could shrug your shoulders. And walk away. But *now* . . . I dunno. Soon as it leaks I'm sure they'll be looking for —

B: What if we sold it as candy?

A: Candy?

B: Candy. Y'know . . .

A: You mean . . .

B: We'd outsource it.

A: Candy.

B: Ship it overseas.

A: Have it . . .

B: Get it processed. A thin, a a viscous . . .

A: Wrap it in . . . in individually wrapped . . .

B: Market it toward children. *(Beat.)* Well?

A: How would it taste?

B: We'd add artificial flavors.

A: Would there be sprinkles?

B: There could be sprinkles.

A: What color sprinkles?

B: Whatever color you want.

A: It would be the rage!

B: *(Beat.)* Of course . . .

A: What?

B: Well, there would be a . . . a certain amount of . . . contempt.

A: Oh come on: They'd love it, the bastards!

B: There'd be condemnation.

A: But they'd eat it up!

B: They would, wouldn't they.

A: Eat it up, shit it out, eat it again!

B: It could be huge!

A: *(Referring to the box.)* We'd have to go Back Into Production!
   (Pause.)

B: Although . . . The shit . . .

A: What?

B: The shit they shit out.

A: Yeah?

B: Well . . . I mean, it . . . it would . . . We'd have to decontaminate it,
   wouldn't we?

A: "We"?

B: What?

A: "We"? *(Beat.)* We'll be *dead!*

B: God, you're right!

A: Time they notice, we'll be *long* dead.

B: And they'll figure something out.

A: Look: They're very innovative.

B: Yes.

A: Very . . .

B: They are.

A: Oh, they're extraordinarily . . .

B: Who?

A: People.

B: *Ah.*

A: Aren't they? *(Beat.)* And the one where he goes and lives with the nuns.

B: Yes.

A: In Harlem.

B: Fantastic.

A: Remember it?

B: Oh I've committed it to memory.

A: God, I get a kick outta that one.

END OF PLAY

BRUSHSTROKE

JOHN SHANAHAN

Brushstroke was first performed as part of the Boston Theater Marathon, May 2006. It was produced by TYG Productions. The cast was: Timothy Parsons — Vincent Ernest Siders; Gavin Taylor — Jeff Gill. Directed by Vincent Ernest Siders.

CHARACTERS

TIMOTHY PARSONS, an artist, mid-twenties to early fifties
GAVIN TAYLOR, his friend and/or patron, thirties to forties

SETTING

Artist's studio

•   •   •

Scene: Gavin Taylor, a neatly dressed man in his thirties to forties, stands at C, looking with some degree of awe over a large contemporary painting. (The painting's presence at C front should only be suggested.) It's a modern piece, many bold swaths and smaller strokes across the canvas. To anyone but Timothy, it would appear quite finished. To one side is a small table holding a palette with blobs of paint on it and several brushes. Upstage, slouched in a chair rubbing his eyes, is Timothy Parsons, the artist. He can be any age from late-twenties to fifties. He's dressed in a casual, artsy style, but his clothes are not the paint-spattered kind typically used to say "artist." He hasn't painted in so much as a dot in the last three weeks.

GAVIN: My. Timothy, oh my.
TIM: *(Without looking.)* Mm hmm.
GAVIN: This is . . . magnificent.
TIM: Hmm.
GAVIN: I mean it's — I hate to sound gushy, but . . . it's so powerful. Stunning.
TIM: You think so, huh?
GAVIN: *(Crossing back toward Tim.)* I really do.
TIM: Huh.
GAVIN: Don't you think so?
TIM: I wouldn't know.
GAVIN: *(Laughing.)* The artist wouldn't know if his work was good?
TIM: *(Flatly.)* It's hard to say until it's finished.
   (Pause. Gavin looks at Tim, then to the painting, then back to Tim.)
GAVIN: It's not done?
TIM: *(With some exhaustion.)* No. It's not done.
GAVIN: Really? Because, you know, it honestly is quite —
TIM: It's not done.
   (A tense pause.)
GAVIN: You could have fooled me.

TIM: Apparently I did.

GAVIN: Not done.

TIM: No.

GAVIN: How much longer do you figure before it is?

TIM: Hard to say.

GAVIN: How long has it been like this? Unfinished.

TIM: Three weeks, maybe.

GAVIN: Ah. *(He takes a few steps back and studies the painting.)* You've made a good start.

TIM: Very funny.

GAVIN: So what is it missing? What is it going to take to finish it?

TIM: One brushstroke.

> *(Silence. Gavin looks at Timothy with a question on his lips.)*

TIM: One brushstroke. Then it's done.

GAVIN: Are you serious?

TIM: *(Crossing past him to regard the painting.)* Quite.

GAVIN: So you could finish it today. Now.

TIM: No.

GAVIN: No?

> *(Timothy looks at the painting. Cocks his head. Shakes his head and walks back to the chair and sits wearily.)*

TIM: No.

GAVIN: You're beginning to worry me, Timothy.

TIM: Imagine how I feel.

> *(Pause. Gavin regards Timothy, as if to gauge if he's serious. To some degree, Gavin feels that he's not. He picks up a brush from the table, walks back to Timothy, and holds it out to him.)*

GAVIN: Finish it. *(Pause.)* Come on, just finish it, then we'll go have a drink to celebrate. I'm buying.

TIM: Just like that?

GAVIN: Come on. One brushstroke and be done with it!

TIM: Where does it go? *(Pause.)* If it's so patently simple, Gavin, then help me out here. Where is it supposed to go?

GAVIN: It's not my work.

TIM: No, no, no, no — you don't back out like that. You don't just merrily tell me to pick up my brush and finish my painting and then say you don't know how.

GAVIN: But I —

TIM: Come on! Tell me where it goes! Tell me how to finish it! *(He snatches the brush from Gavin and waves it at the canvas.)* Does it go here? Huh? Up in this corner? No? The middle? Where, Gavin? Show me exactly where! How long should it be? How wide? Do you know? And what color? Is it brown? Is it sort of brown? Is it blue, Gavin? Is it? What if it's not blue, Gavin? What then? WHAT IF IT'S NOT SUPPOSED TO BE BLUE? *(He throws the brush down, storms across stage, and kicks the chair. He stands with his back to Gavin.)*

(A lengthy, tense silence.)

GAVIN: I didn't want — I meant no disrespect, Timothy.

TIM: I know.

GAVIN: Do you want to talk about it?

(Timothy thinks a moment. He crosses to the brush, wherever it is, picks it up and puts it back on the table with the palette.)

TIM: Probably. And I probably should. But to tell you the truth, I'm not sure I'd know what to say.

GAVIN: Just tell me what's going on.

(Timothy turns and smiles at him, but it's a sharp smile, almost a smirk.)

TIM: That's what I like about you, Gavin. You have this firm, simple belief in the absolute black and whiteness of things. You genuinely believe that whatever's happening with me not finishing this can just be drawn out somehow by you asking me what's going on. That there's got to be this one thing that constitutes the entire problem.

GAVIN: *(Simply.)* Isn't there?

(Pause.)

GAVIN: Has anyone else seen this?

TIM: No.

GAVIN: Then why is it so bothersome that I, being the first person to find out that one brushstroke has kept you from finishing a great painting, should ask what's wrong?

TIM: I never said bothersome —

GAVIN: Then what?

TIM: It's not that simple!

GAVIN: Why?

TIM: Why do you need to know?

(Gavin laughs.)

GAVIN: Because you're my friend, Timothy. Because I come here and I find you in this mood, with this problem, and — I'm honestly surprised that you have to ask me why I need to know! Why couldn't you have just said it's not done and left it at that? Or told me that it *was* done? Or hidden the damn thing in the first place?

(Timothy is at a loss.)

GAVIN: Because you couldn't. Because you needed someone to know. You wanted someone to ask. Here I am.

TIM: Here you are.

GAVIN: And I'm asking.

TIM: Yes you are.

(Another silence. Gavin is determined to ride it out, to have Timothy speak first. After several beats, Timothy sighs.)

TIM: Would you say, Gavin, that this is the best work I've ever done?

GAVIN: I'd have to say it's definitely on par with —

TIM: If you want to help me, Gavin, then answer the question. And it's a yes or no question. Is this the best work I've ever done?

GAVIN: You say it's not done.

TIM: You didn't know that when you first saw it. You told me it was stunning.

GAVIN: Well it is!

TIM: So is this my best work?

GAVIN: Yes. Probably.

TIM: Probably means no.

GAVIN: All right. Yes.

TIM: Exactly.

GAVIN: Exactly *what?*

TIM: This may very well be my best.

GAVIN: Well, then, congratulations!

(Pause. A short, sad laugh from Timothy.)

TIM: I don't know why I thought you'd see it. I don't — *(He's at a loss. He throws his hands up.)*

GAVIN: What? *(He throws his hands up, mocking Timothy.)* What is *this?*

(A moment where Timothy's anger builds. Then he storms to the canvas.)

TIM: This *is* my best painting. And the minute I take up that brush and I put that one final smear of paint, that line, that dot, whatever it is that finishes it, on that canvas, I will be *expected* to create another one that is better than this. My best. *(Calming in voice but not in mindset.)* If I finish this right now, then tomorrow or the next day or a year from now there will be a blank canvas — waiting — and from the first brushstroke, the first choice of color, it has to be better than this. But it has to come from somewhere. What if I don't have anything left after this?

GAVIN: Timothy. Really. This is just not sensible. This is just some sort of artistic post-partum depression. Art is a birthing process. I know that. You carry it around, you nurture it, and when it's done you have to separate from it, and I understand that can be difficult. Timothy, you're a brilliant artist. You don't need to worry that you won't have another idea.

TIM: "Idea." Your understanding is that this is me worrying about having an idea.

GAVIN: *(Smiling.)* Correct me if I'm wrong.

(Pause, as Timothy debates whether to go forward.)

TIM: I started planning this painting eleven months ago. At the time, I thought it was simply going to be my next painting. Just my next one. But as I worked on it, I knew it was becoming something, but not like before. I became very particular about it. And I got to this point, where it is now. Really about eight months of actual work — sketching, painting, refining everything. One morning I came out to work and . . . I saw something. I saw every day of those eight months, all tied together on the canvas. I saw moments. I looked into it, I touched it. I started to think about what each pass of the brush meant. I wondered. Where were the bits that I painted when I was happy? When I was pissed off? Where I was invigorated? Where I was frustrated? What parts did I paint in the day? Which were those ones where I woke up in the middle of the night just knowing that I had to paint — those ideas that just come and won't go away? Where were the things that I'd painted over? What had *they* meant, where had *they* come from? Where did all of *this* come from?

(Pause.)

And then, in this one moment, I understood. In one way or another, I put everything I am *(Touching the canvas.)* here. Almost everything. *(Without turning.)* And I am scared, Gavin, scared to death to think that when I put that one final stroke on this canvas, that I will have finally given everything that I am, and that it will be all that I have. I am afraid, Gavin, that in a very real way, I will disappear.

GAVIN: Nothing left, or nothing left to give?

TIM: They're the same.

GAVIN: Don't you wonder, though?

TIM: Wonder what?

GAVIN: What comes next, of course.

TIM: Yes, I do. And it scares the shit out of me.

GAVIN: Then it must be art.

TIM: What?

(Gavin picks up the palette and brush.)

GAVIN: One brushstroke. Then there's either something or there's nothing. But either way, there's art. Which is more than most people can say. Eight months you worked on this?

TIM: Yes.

GAVIN: Then what's one more day's work?

(He holds the palette out to Timothy. Pause.)

GAVIN: Not knowing will kill you.

(A beat. Timothy reluctantly steps over toward Gavin. He looks at the painting, then takes the palette. He turns back to the canvas, staring intently into it.)

GAVIN: Do you mind if I watch?

TIM: *(Snapping his attention away.)* What?

GAVIN: Can I watch you finish it?

TIM: Certainly. Yes. Please.

(Timothy hesitates. He looks at the palette, the brush poised above it. Then, without turning:)

TIM: Gavin?

GAVIN: Yes?

TIM: What color is the last part of my soul?

GAVIN: *(After a beat.)* Timothy, you've known what color it is for the last three weeks.

(Timothy turns and looks at him.)

GAVIN: Paint it.

(Timothy turns back, and looks once more at the palette. He begins mixing colors as the lights fade.)

END OF PLAY

Cave Krewe

KARA LEE CORTHRON

Cave Krewe was produced by manhattantheatresource in
Week 3 of Estrogenius 2006 (Fiona Jones, Founder & Execu-
tive Producer), more info at www.theatresource.org.
Cast: Rodney — Keith Chappelle; Benjamin — Christopher
Burris. Director: Heidi Handelsman;
Producer: Shoshona Currier.

CHARACTERS

RODNEY, African-American, a very mature thirteen
BENJAMIN, African-American, a very young twelve, who talks very fast
*Both actors are to be adults that can play children

SETTING

An outdoor area near the opening of a cave in suburban Maryland

TIME

February 28, 2006, after school

•   •   •

Rodney stands outside, not far from the cave. He wears headphones. He carefully takes the attached discman from his backpack and holds it delicately. He takes out a large bottle of soda and begins to drink it down. Benjamin enters and stares at Rodney. He drinks almost the whole bottle before noticing Benjamin. Rodney stops drinking.

RODNEY: *Shit!*

BENJAMIN: What're you doing here? The *cave?* Spooky up here!

RODNEY: D'you follow me here, ya freak?

BENJAMIN: Ya know, you aren't suppose to drink soda straight from the bottle! It's unsanitary. If you were to share it now, whoever you share it with would get your germs and whoever's germs you got from drinking behind anybody else *you* mighta drank behind. And it's real bad for your teeth. You can get cavities from the sugar and then you have to go to the dentist and the dentist fills a hole and gives you a filling and — um a — now dentists can give you fillings that are white so they match your teeth and nobody even knows you have'em — um a — unless your teeth are yellow or brown. Then they have to—

(Rodney throws the remainder of his soda in Benjamin's face. Benjamin is silent.)

RODNEY: Happy Mardi Gras, bizatch!

BENJAMIN: Why did you do that? Ya didn't have to do that! That's not a happy-Mardi-Gras thing to do!

RODNEY: 'Cuz you a yackin' machine!

(As Benjamin tries to clean himself off, Rodney starts to put his discman away.)

BENJAMIN: *Hey!* That's all that is? I know we're not supposed to ask too many personal things 'cuz then you guys might get annoyed, but — um a —

Why're you always hiding it in your bag? I thought it was — um a — an iPod or something really expensive 'cuz you act it's gonna get stolen and I — um a — don't think anybody cares about some old CD player.

RODNEY: My mother told me to never let nobody touch this player and I promised her and I will *not*.

BENJAMIN: Ohhh. So, it's from your —

RODNEY: Whatchu want, little man? Make sure I got all my homework assignments written down? I do. See if I need ta join yer ma's carpool? I don't. Find out if I'll sign up for the after-school soccer league? I won't. I can't see no other reason why you need to be followin' me anywhere, so why dontchu get ta steppin,' goody-goody.

BENJAMIN: No! I'm supposed ta — I have to just make sure you're doin' OK. That you aren't gettin' into . . . trouble.

RODNEY: Checkin' up on yer little project? Bad enough they make you find me 'tween every single class. Now you gon' start stalkin' me on my own time?

BENJAMIN: I take the welcoming committee very seriously and sometimes my duties go beyond the normal school day. It is my job to make sure you are — um a — happy and well-adjusted. So—

RODNEY: Bullshit.

BENJAMIN: I'm going to ignore that!

You don't wanna go in the cave. It's haunted. Dead twins. Car accident. Spooky stuff.

RODNEY: That don't scare me.

(*Pause.*)

BENJAMIN: What d'ya wanna do in there? In the — um a — cave?

RODNEY: Get good and toasted. Why not?

BENJAMIN: You mean abuse drugs?

RODNEY: No, I'mma jump in a toaster! Use ya head, son!

BENJAMIN: Instead of doing *that*, you can come over to my house. For a little while. Before you have to go home to your cousin's for dinner.

(*Pause.*)

OR you can eat dinner with us.

RODNEY: Whatchall eatin'?

BENJAMIN: Tuna casserole.

RODNEY: Thank you *no!*

BENJAMIN: What did you used to eat in Louisiana? Crayfish . . . casserole?

RODNEY: You talk too much.

BENJAMIN: Sorry. So, ya wanna just come over and play — I mean, hang?

RODNEY: Boy, hold old you think I am?

BENJAMIN: About — um a — eleven?

RODNEY: *Eleven?* I'm in the eighth grade!

BENJAMIN: I know but how comes I'm taller than you then? Explain that! I'm taller than you and I'm only in seventh grade! In health class we learned that if you don't — um a — hit you're growth spurt by a certain age, you'll never have one and you'll just be a short man. Sometimes, if you're real short — like you are — you might have to go to a doctor 'cuz you might have this disease called —

RODNEY: MAN! Will you just shut your mouth?!

BENJAMIN: No.

RODNEY: Go home! I ain't interested in playin' Barbies with you!

BENJAMIN: Who TOLD you that?

RODNEY: What?

BENJAMIN: It's not true! I only ever play with my Yu-Gi-Oh Amphibian Beast, Bazoo the Soul-Eater, and Fire Princess trading cards. Or my Yugi action figure! I *swear* it! Anything else you heard was a lie.
(*Pause.*)

RODNEY: Aight, man.

BENJAMIN: Good.

RODNEY: So go on home and play wit yer nerdy crap.

BENJAMIN: But — I just thought you should have some company. Today.

RODNEY: How lonely *are* you?
(*Pause.*)

BENJAMIN: I'm here to help *you*.

RODNEY: I am officially refusing yer help.

BENJAMIN: OK. Um a — I guess I'll leave you alone then.
(*Benjamin starts to walk away and then hides. Rodney turns to walk into the cave. Suddenly, Benjamin runs up and tackles him.*)

RODNEY: What the *FUCK* are you doing?

BENJAMIN: Don't worry, Rodney! It's for your own good!
(*Benjamin wrestles Rodney's backpack away from him.*)

RODNEY: If this is some kinda gay thing, I am really not cool with it, yo!
(*Benjamin empties the bag of its contents.*)

BENJAMIN: Oh. There's nothing in here.

RODNEY: What the FUCK is yer problem?

BENJAMIN: You say "fuck" a lot.

RODNEY: ANSWER ME!

BENJAMIN: OK! I heard you talking today and I had to make sure you didn't have anything! Like an exacto knife from the art room or some kinda poison from the janitor's closet. Like anything — dangerous.

RODNEY: WHAT?

BENJAMIN: Dangerous to your*self.* You said something weird at lunch to Mrs. Finkle. You said this was your last day to have a good time so you better enjoy it while it lasts. I was scared you were gonna . . . that you might try to . . . ya know?

(Benjamin makes the gesture of cutting his throat along with the sound effect.)

She told me you were probably fine. But *I* decided to check out your bag and call her cell phone if there was anything dangerous in it.

RODNEY: Why would you think that?

BENJAMIN: Well, you're usually pretty grumpy and depressed. And you *said:* It's your last day!? Enjoy it while it lasts! Isn't that what you said? Why did you say that?

(Rodney thinks. He laughs.)

RODNEY: No, dumbass! Why you think I was drinkin' all that pop before? It's *Fat Tuesday!* Mardi Gras! Like I said! Dontchu even know what that means?

(Benjamin stares blankly.)

I meant today's the last day to have a ball before lent! Y'all some heathens up here! Don't know jack 'bout no real Christian customs!

BENJAMIN: So . . . ?

RODNEY: So *nothin'!* I ain't doin' nothin,' but a little celebratin' 'fore tomorra! That was all I meant! Jesus!

BENJAMIN: Oh.

(Pause.)

In that case, wanna come over to my house to celebrate?

RODNEY: NO! An' since I ain't ready to do myself in, you can go now.

(Benjamin is hurt; he doesn't move.)

RODNEY: 'Sides, you too young for me to hang out with. I can't figure for shit why they paired me with you. Not a good match.

BENJAMIN: I'm only a year younger.

RODNEY: In life experience, I'm yer dad.

BENJAMIN: Huh?

RODNEY: See? It's the truth.

(Pause.)

You got some balls to tackle somebody like that, man.

BENJAMIN: I do?

RODNEY: You play football?

BENJAMIN: Asthma.

RODNEY: Oh.

(Pause.)

BENJAMIN: What — um a — what CD you been listenin' to?

RODNEY: *The New Danger.* You like Mos Def?

BENJAMIN: Yeah. He's pretty cool.

RODNEY: Ya know who he is?

BENJAMIN: Sure. Well, no.

> *(Rodney hesitates then puts the headphones on Benjamin's head. Benjamin nods, listens. His expression reveals that he can't decide if he likes it or not. After a minute, he hands them back to Rodney.)*

RODNEY: Not yer style?

BENJAMIN: I don't know. I don't know too much rap music. But I have this midget uncle in jail for gettin' in a gang fight. He's in California. He likes rap.

RODNEY: OK.

BENJAMIN: We have a block on our cable so we can't watch MTV or BET.

RODNEY: Ya listen to the radio?

BENJAMIN: Gram think the radio is just one big, dirty commercial. She won't let us turn it on.

RODNEY: What kinda music do *you* like?

BENJAMIN: Um a — Can I just not tell you? All you'd do is make fun a me so I'd just like to not even tell you.

RODNEY: I won't make fun a ya. I don't care enough to make fun a ya.

BENJAMIN: I bet you will.

RODNEY: Uh-uh.

> *(Pause.)*

BENJAMIN: The Mamas and the Papas. And Fifth Dimension. The Cowsills. Gram's records.

> Do you know those guys?

RODNEY: No. Is that like the old school joints?

BENJAMIN: Yeah. I think so.

> I do like your discman. You're smart to keep it safe. Hidden away. I don't think I've ever seen it before today. Sony?
>
> *(Rodney shrugs.)*

BENJAMIN: Panasonic?

> *(Rodney shrugs.)*
>
> Well, can I see it?
>
> *(Benjamin reaches for the discman. Rodney snatches it away and pushes Benjamin away violently.)*

RODNEY: I *told* you: Nobody. Nobody touches my discman. But me. You understand?

> *(Benjamin stares at him.)*

BENJAMIN: Sorry. I was just — um a — tryin' to find out the brand. No big deal. I know you really like it. I know your mom gave it to you. I won't try to touch it again.

RODNEY: You tryna mess with me?

BENJAMIN: No.

(Rodney holds the player close to him, hugging it. He turns to go into the cave.)

BENJAMIN: Have you talked to your mom? Yet?

(Rodney turns, runs to Benjamin, and grabs him by his collar.)

RODNEY: Looky here, you little fuck: My mother is fine! I keep tellin' you meddlin' assholes this over and over! Stop with the goddamn questions and the sympathy. You make we wanna puke! My mother is NOT hurt! And she sure ain't DEAD! She is fine. She is *fine*. It is a big city, we from. She just got stuck somewhere. Lotsa corners to get stuck in now. She might be in Houston. She might be in Jackson. She could be in a whole lotta places, OK? You don't know! Right now — I can see her in my mind — she is sippin' on a daiquiri and laughin' and tellin' the stupid story a how she got separated from me, Lou and Dad and got trapped on a bus or on a rooftop and had to get rescued by some musclehead in a uniform. She is *enjoyin'* her Fat Tuesday just like I'm fittin' ta do. She's dancin' at the Zulu Krewe parade like last year and every year since forever! And the *only* reason I ain't heard from her yet is 'cuz she just ain't called the right person. We got tons a family, but she ain't figured out that I'm with Dad's cousin, Pam. An' it might take her awhile to figure that out.

And she prolly don't even have her address book with her. So you see? My mother is fine. She's just a little stuck right now. Don't ask questions about her again. Got it?

BENJAMIN: Got it.

(Rodney lets go of Benjamin. Silence.)

BENJAMIN: *(Carefully:)* Of course she's fine. I wouldna asked otherwise.

RODNEY: *What?*

BENJAMIN: I *know* she's fine. You're the one that's so worried about everything. That's why Mrs. Finkle wants me around you so much. But you don't have to worry. Wherever she's at, your mom is doing OK. I just have that feeling, ya know?

(Pause.)

RODNEY: Ya do?

BENJAMIN: Well, sure! Don't you?

(Another pause.)

RODNEY: Yeah! 'Course I do, man.
Um — Thanks, Ben.

BENJAMIN: You remembered my name?

(Rodney nods and starts toward the cave again. He hesitates.)

RODNEY: You — wan' come with me?

BENJAMIN: *Me?* In there? Don't you think I'm too young?

RODNEY: Yep. But knowledge has to come *some*time. Come on.

(Rodney starts in. Benjamin hesitates, thinks about it. Then:)

BENJAMIN: OK. Last day to have a good time, right? And — um a — maybe it's only haunted at night. Ya think?

RODNEY: Whatever. You ain't *smokin*,' though. Way too young for that. But you can hang wit me. For a little while. You bess not snitch.

(Benjamin shakes his head. As they walk into the cave:)

RODNEY: You ain't the onliest one to play wit Barbies, ya know?

BENJAMIN: NO WAY! *You* played with 'em?

RODNEY: Sure. This game my brother made up called "anatomical corrections." You know about it?

BENJAMIN: Uh-uh.

RODNEY: You strip alla Barbie's clothes off. You take a permanent marker and— ya know them big titties Barbie's been blessed wit? They sorta missin' an important part.

BENJAMIN: They *are?*

RODNEY: Boy, you get younger by the minute.

(They exit into the cave. Silence. We hear the sound of a match striking. Then:)

BENJAMIN: Um a — Is there gonna be second-hand smoke?

END OF PLAY

COCKTAIL CONVERSATION

ANDREW BISS

Cocktail Conversation ran September 21 to October 8, 2006, as part of an evening of one-act plays entitled: *Biss-ous: Four One-Act Plays by Andrew Biss* at the Théâtre Ste. Catherine in Montréal, Quebec, Canada. It was produced by: Unwashed Grape Productions (Laura Mitchell, Co-Artistic Director, Paul Hawkins, Co-Artistic Director). The cast: Jim — Toma Weideman; Mike — Nathaniel Amranian.

CHARACTERS

MIKE, amiable. Not as confident as he'd like to appear. Good-looking. Early to mid-twenties.

JIM, mordant sense of humor. Somewhat jaded in attitude. Good-looking. Early to mid-twenties.

SETTING

A bar in a gay nightclub

TIME

Night. The present.

.   .   .

Two young men sit at a bar in a gay nightclub, each cradling a glass in his hands. Both appear less than enthused as they idly observe the various people who come and go before them at a point somewhere beyond the fourth wall. As each unseen patron passes their field of view — from left to right and visa versa — their heads follow, sometimes in unison, as they offer their critiques.

MIKE: *(His eyes following someone across the room.)* Done him.
JIM: Done him.
    (Pause. Another passerby crosses their view.)
MIKE: Done him.
JIM: Yep, done him.
    (Pause. Another passerby crosses their view.)
MIKE: Done him, as well.
JIM: Yeah, done him, too.
    (Pause. Another passerby crosses their view.)
MIKE: I've *definitely* done him.
JIM: Who hasn't done him?
    (Pause. Mike takes something from his shirt pocket and puts it in his mouth, swallows it, and washes down with a swig from his glass. Another passerby crosses their view.)
MIKE: Not sure if I've done him.
    (Beat.)
    Looks familiar, though.
JIM: I've done him.
MIKE: Have you?
JIM: Oh, yeah. Done him not long ago, as a matter of fact.

MIKE: Have I done him?

JIM: How should I know? Ask him.

MIKE: Think I've done him . . . I'm just not sure.

> (Beat.)

> Well, you've done him — if I haven't done him should I do him?

JIM: *(With a shrug.)* Up to you. Personally I wouldn't do him again.

MIKE: Mmm.

> (Pause. This time Jim takes something from his shirt pocket and puts it in his mouth, swallows it, and washes down with a swig from his glass. Another passerby crosses their view.)

MIKE: Now, I've done *him* a few times.

JIM: I done him once, but . . . God knows when. Years ago, that's for sure.

MIKE: One time five of us did him at once.

JIM: Tight squeeze.

MIKE: Very funny.

JIM: That explains it, then.

MIKE: Explains what?

JIM: Why he walks like that.

MIKE: Like what?

JIM: Like Donald Duck.

MIKE: No, he always walked like that. I think he thinks it makes people think he's got a big cock.

JIM: Does he?

MIKE: 'Course not, that's why he does it. If there was truth in advertising he'd be pigeon-toed.

JIM: You'd think I'd remember, wouldn't you? Aren't I awful?

MIKE: Aren't we all?

> (Pause. Mike, again, takes something from his shirt pocket and puts it in his mouth, swallows it, and washes down with a swig from his glass. Another passerby crosses their view.)

JIM: *(Mischievously.)* Have you done him?

MIKE: *(Beat.)* I don't remember.

JIM: So you have done him?

MIKE: I said I don't remember.

> (Beat.)

> And if I have done him it was probably because I was depressed . . . and bored . . . and couldn't find anything to wear that made me feel attractive to the same sex . . . and 'cause I looked in the mirror that morning and saw the first signs of my face losing its natural elasticity . . . and 'cause I'd left my contact lenses in the cleaning solution too long which meant

I couldn't wear them that night which meant I was half blind . . . and 'cause that day that bitch Janice at work told me I looked like I was "filling out" which was her way of saying I looked like a fat pig who'd be more at home stuck on a spit roasting over an open fire, which completely sapped my confidence and is exactly where she should be, with the flames licking up around those ugly Ann Taylor business suits she prances around in!

(Beat.)

But . . . like I say . . . I'm not saying I have done him — I just don't remember.

JIM: (Gleefully.) I *knew* it!

MIKE: And you haven't?

JIM: Sorry, dreamboat, you're on your own there.

(Beat.)

Oh, no.

MIKE: What?

JIM: Your old shag — look what she's doing.

MIKE: Oh, no.

JIM: If she thinks for one second that bumming a light from Mr. Pecs is going to land her a night in Studsville she is sadly mistaken.

MIKE: *Sadly* mistaken.

JIM: Doomed to failure.

MIKE: Doomed.

(Pause.)

JIM: (Fatalistically.) There . . . blown off like a wet sperm fart.

MIKE: Some people just have no concept of what league they belong in.

JIM: Perhaps she was hoping Mr. Pecs had forgotten his contacts.

MIKE: I said I don't remember — remember?

JIM: Mmm . . . well, I'll say this much for her, she obviously manages to save money by not spending on clothes.

MIKE: Mmm . . . or matches.

JIM: Mmm.

(Pause. Mike, again, takes something from his shirt pocket and puts it in his mouth, swallows it, and washes down with a swig from his glass. Another passerby crosses their view.)

MIKE: Done him.

JIM: Of course you've done him — everyone's done him. I wouldn't be surprised if he hasn't done himself.

MIKE: I did him once with his girlfriend watching.

JIM: Girlfriend?

MIKE: Yeah, back when he was, you know . . . trying to pass.

JIM: Pass as what?

MIKE: Who knows?

JIM: What could you possibly pass as with a hair-do like that?

MIKE: Search me.

JIM: A former member of Duran Duran, maybe?

MIKE: Possibly.

JIM: And what did she think?

MIKE: Who?

JIM: The girlfriend.

MIKE: Couldn't tell you. She was completely strung out on . . . something. All I remember is her snapping her fingers out of time and singing the chorus of "Love Is a Battlefield" over and over again.

JIM: Pat Benatar?

MIKE: Mmm.

JIM: Sad.

MIKE: Sad.

(Pause. Another passerby crosses their view.)

JIM: Done him.

MIKE: Yep, done him.

(Pause. Jim, again, takes something from his shirt pocket and puts it in his mouth, swallows it, and washes down with a swig from his glass. Another passerby crosses their view.)

MIKE: Done that one.

JIM: *(With great scepticism.)* Yeah!

MIKE: What do you mean by that?

JIM: I mean, "Yeah!"

MIKE: Are you calling me a liar?

JIM: Not a *liar*, no, but . . . that's Miss Love Story.

MIKE: Who?

JIM: Miss "I won't have sex with anyone unless it means something."

MIKE: Well, *I* had sex with him.

JIM: Perhaps she's in love with you?

MIKE: So you *are* calling me a liar?

JIM: Look, I just know for a fact that she won't have sex with just anyone.

MIKE: Me being "just anyone"?

JIM: Of course you are. So am I. And I know from experience that she's extremely picky.

MIKE: Too picky to pick me according to you.

JIM: Maybe.

MIKE: Well, maybe you should make a note of this, Mr. Love Story-less: *That* is his routine.

JIM: What is?

MIKE: That whole, "It has to mean something to me" routine; just like my, "Oh, you seemed so straight-looking, I thought you must've come here by mistake" routine, and your, "I'm actually married with three kids at home, but don't tell anyone" routine. It's how he operates.

JIM: Oh . . . huh!

(Beat.)

Sorry.

MIKE: Half-hearted apology accepted.

(Pause. Mike, again, takes something from his shirt pocket and puts it in his mouth, swallows it, and washes down with a swig from his glass. Another passerby crosses their view.)

JIM: Done him, done him, done him, God, I don't know *how* many times! How ever does he find the nerve to show his face down here?

MIKE: The same way you do, I expect.

JIM: I said I was sorry.

MIKE: Apology accepted — again.

(Beat.)

JIM: He has a third nipple, you know.

MIKE: Does he? Where?

JIM: Between his third and fourth ribs on the left-hand side — if you're going upwards.

MIKE: I always go upwards.

(Beat.)

Three nipples . . . fancy that.

JIM: You've never done one with three nipples?

MIKE: Not that I'm aware of.

JIM: It's more common than you'd think.

MIKE: You live and learn, don't you? Could be quite fun, I suppose.

JIM: Well, call me old-fashioned but I still prefer just the two, otherwise I get this weird feeling I'm fucking a distant cousin of The Elephant Man or The Bearded Lady.

MIKE: Listen to you, you old-fashioned softy.

JIM: Bit of a passion killer . . . for me, at least.

MIKE: But only a "bit," apparently.

JIM: Well, I'd spent a long time working on him, hadn't I? — I wasn't about to pack it in just because an extra nipple appeared on the scene. So, I took a deep breath and . . . packed it in.

MIKE: I thought you said you'd done him "God knows how many times"?

JIM: *(With a shrug.)* Well . . . it's like that song, "I've Grown Accustomed to His Face" — I grew accustomed to his extra nipple.

MIKE: That was a sweet thing to say.

JIM: Thank you.

(Pause. Another passerby crosses their view.)

JIM: *(Sympathetically.)* Ahhh . . . poor thing.

MIKE: I know . . . it's sad.

JIM: Still, let's not get down. She'll find someone . . . one of these days.

MIKE: One of these days.

(Pause. Both Mike and Jim take something from their shirt pockets and put it in their mouths, swallow it, and wash it down with a swig from their glasses. Another passerby crosses their view.)

MIKE: *(Affronted.)* Oh, just look at him!

JIM: I am — every bit of him.

MIKE: You know I done him?

JIM: *(In disbelief.)* You did not.

MIKE: Before he was even legal.

JIM: I hate you!

MIKE: Well, don't hate me that much — that was when he was still in his "I'm not sure what I am" phase. It was all very awkward and unsatisfying. Now look at him: the "it man" . . . the belle of the ball. He makes me sick.

JIM: Mmm . . . even so.

MIKE: *(Upon reflection.)* Yeah . . . even so.

(Pause. Another passerby crosses their view.)

JIM: Ooh, look at that. I'd do him in a New York minute.

MIKE: That's all you'd need.

JIM: You've done him?

MIKE: Briefly.

JIM: I don't care. Someone like that, I'd just be happy to bathe my eyes in his beautiful, criminal, physical perfection.

(Beat.)

That, and shove my cock up his ass as hard as I could.

MIKE: You are in a silly, romantic mood this evening, aren't you?

JIM: Must've been all that talk about Miss Love Story.

(Pause. Jim, again, takes something from his shirt pocket and puts it in his mouth, swallows it, and washes down with a swig from his glass. Another passerby crosses their view.)

MIKE: Not if you paid me.

JIM: Not if you paid me either . . . unless it was a lot.

MIKE: What do you call a lot?

JIM: I don't know . . . a lot.

MIKE: Like what?

JIM: A hell of a lot.

MIKE: A thousand?

JIM: Oh, fuck off!

MIKE: Well, what then?

JIM: I don't know.

MIKE: Ten thousand?

JIM: I don't know.

MIKE: A hundred thousand?

JIM: Well, of course a hundred thousand.

MIKE: You'd do that for a hundred thousand?

JIM: You wouldn't?

MIKE: For a hundred thousand . . . probably.

JIM: What do you mean, "probably"? You'd fuck it like it was Tom Cruise if you knew there was a hundred grand at the other end.

MIKE: What end?

JIM: His end.

MIKE: Wouldn't you?

JIM: Of course I would.

MIKE: So, what's your point?

JIM: It was your point.

MIKE: Point taken.

(Pause. Another passerby crosses their view.)

JIM: Done him.

MIKE: Yeah, done him.

(Pause. Jim, again, takes something from his shirt pocket and puts it in his mouth, swallows it, and washes down with a swig from his glass. Another passerby crosses their view.)

MIKE: Done that one, too.

JIM: *(Apathetically.)* Yep, done.

(Pause. Mike, again, takes something from his shirt pocket and puts it in his mouth, swallows it, and washes down with a swig from his glass. Another passerby crosses their view.)

MIKE: Oh, look . . . there's Pork Tenderloin.

JIM: Who?

MIKE: Pork Tenderloin.

JIM: What do you call him that for?

MIKE: Only takes meat if it comes shrink-wrapped in plastic.

JIM: Once upon a time, maybe — not any more. These days he gets it fresh from the butchers.

MIKE: How would you know?

JIM: 'Cause I done him.

MIKE: Shrink-wrapped?

JIM: No.

MIKE: You must've been. He's very fussy. Famous for it.

JIM: *(Emphatically.)* I've done him.

MIKE: Bareback?

JIM: Bareback.

MIKE: Well, either he knows something that you don't know, or I know something that he doesn't know.

JIM: What?

MIKE: Either . . . actually, I'm not sure now. I think I've confused myself.

JIM: Look, it was no big deal, I just explained to him that if he'd never done it skinless then he'd never *really* done it 'cause it feels completely different, and that, anyway, it doesn't really matter who's positive and who's not these days, 'cause whatever happens — with the right drug combo — you can virtually live forever.

MIKE: Then he said yes?

JIM: Then he said, "Who'd wanna do that?"

MIKE: What a funny thing to say. Was he depressed?

JIM: Couldn't tell you.

MIKE: So, then you did him?

JIM: Then I did him.

MIKE: Skinless.

JIM: But not boneless.

MIKE: Fuck, if I'd known it was that easy I'd have done him long ago.
(Beat.)
Finished your cocktail?

JIM: *(As he reaches into his shirt pocket.)* Two more . . . hang on.
(Jim swallows the last of his pills and takes a swig from his glass, as Mike reaches inside of his own shirt pocket.)

JIM: Finished yours?

MIKE: *(Still feeling about in his pocket.)* Yep . . . nope . . . one more.
(Mike swallows his last pill and washes it down with a swig from his glass.)

JIM: See anything worth doing?

MIKE: Not tonight.

JIM: Got your contacts in?

MIKE: Yeah.

JIM: Wanna do me?

MIKE: Might as well.

(Mike and Jim get up to leave.)

JIM: Aren't you going to finish your water?

MIKE: I don't like water.

JIM: Please yourself.

(Mike and Jim begin to leave. Mike suddenly stops.)

MIKE: Wait . . . my cigarettes.

(Mike steps back to the bar and retrieves his cigarettes.)

JIM: I thought you were giving that up, anyway?

MIKE: I am . . . just not yet.

JIM: *(With a shrug.)* Your funeral.

(They exit as the lights fade to blackout.)

(Curtain.)

END OF PLAY

NORMAL

Jami Brandli

Normal was originally produced by Alarm Clock Theatre at
The Stanford Calderwood Pavilion at the Boston Center for the
Arts. The play premiered as part of the Boston Theater
Marathon VIII on May 21, 2006. Luke Dennis directed the
following cast: Robert — Kevin LeVelle;
Bobby Jr.: Joey DelPonte.

CHARACTERS

> ROBERT, a man, late thirties, somewhat overweight. He's sloppily dressed in a nice suit and tie.
>
> BOBBY JR., Robert's son. A boy, ten, also sloppily dressed in nice clothes. In addition, Bobby Jr. has about ten to fifteen scarves tied around his arms, legs, waist and head. The scarves are bright and colorful.

SETTING

> Late morning. A backyard with a massive old tree.

*AUTHOR'S NOTE

> A tall ladder can be used in lieu of a tree. Keep in mind this exposes Bobby Jr. completely, including all of his scarves. This will give the play a more comedic feel at the start.

• • •

Lights up on a massive old tree. We mostly see the trunk and some leaves. Robert (late thirties), sloppily dressed in a nice suit and tie, runs on stage. He looks at the tree and slowly approaches. He peers up, looking for someone. This someone is Bobby Jr. (ten), his son. We don't fully see Bobby Jr., but his voice is loud and clear.)

ROBERT: Bobby? Bobby Jr. I can see your foot. Come down now.

BOBBY JR.: No.

ROBERT: I said come down.

BOBBY JR.: No.

ROBERT: We're late for brunch with Nana and Grandpa.

BOBBY JR.: I don't care.

ROBERT: But you haven't seen them in months.

BOBBY JR.: I don't care.

ROBERT: "I don't care." "No." Do you know any other words?

BOBBY JR.: Yes.

> *(A moment.)*

ROBERT: Well. What are they?

BOBBY JR.: Leave me alone.

ROBERT: Unbelievable. Your mother is going to be mad, you know. She looks forward to family get-togethers like this and you're making us late.
> *(Beat)*
> Alright. Look. I'm sorry I got mad at you. Really. I didn't mean to yell

like I did. But Bobby, you cannot go outside dressed like you are right now. I'm not saying that you're not normal. You can dress how you are when you're *inside* the house. You just can't go *outside* the house.

BOBBY JR.: Why not?

ROBERT: It's distracting. Not to me. But to other people, I mean.

(Beat)

Will you come down now? Please?

BOBBY JR.: Who?

ROBERT: Who what?

BOBBY JR.: Who am I distracting?

ROBERT: Well. Your fifth grade teacher for one. She said that you're actually distracting your entire class. Apparently, you've been sneaking them out of the house by hiding them in your book bag and then, during your morning recess, you put every single one of them on. I'd say that might be a tad distracting.

BOBBY JR.: Mrs. Walters never said anything to me.

ROBERT: Mrs. Walters probably thought it was best if I talked to you about this. It's sort of a delicate matter.

BOBBY JR.: Why?

ROBERT: Why is it a delicate matter?

BOBBY JR.: Why am I distracting?

ROBERT: *(Looks at watch)* Listen. We can talk about this on the ride over to the restaurant . . .

BOBBY JR.: No . . .

ROBERT: Your grandparents are probably sitting at the table wondering if we're OK. They don't have a cell phone—

BOBBY JR.: I DON'T CARE!

(Robert is a bit startled by his son's outburst, then regains composure and becomes irritated.)

ROBERT: Fine. You want to know why you're distracting? I'll tell you. But you're not going to like it.

(Looks up at the tree)

If I tell you, will you come down?

BOBBY JR.: Yeah.

ROBERT: The way you dress . . . You see, Bobby, the way you're dressing . . . It's not normal for a ten-year-old boy to wear his mother's scarves.

BOBBY JR.: But you said that I am normal.

ROBERT: You are normal. That's just it, you see? You're a normal boy who's walking around wearing his mother's scarves and for some reason, people are distracted by this image. Bobby Jr. is normal and his mother's scarves are normal, right? But if you put the two together, you get distracting.

BOBBY JR.: I don't get it.

ROBERT: Bobby, you're wearing like fifteen scarves at a time. They're tied around your neck and your arms and your waist and your head and your thighs . . . You look like a gypsy. And a ten-year-old gypsy boy walking around suburban America in the twenty-first century is not normal.

BOBBY JR.: I don't believe you.

ROBERT: You don't believe me? OK. Fine. Your mother says you should be entitled to your own opinion, so fine. But I gave you an answer and that means you have to come down. A deal's a deal.

BOBBY JR.: I want to wear Mom's scarves to brunch.

ROBERT: No way. I'm not in the mood answer questions like "Robert, why are you letting my grandson walk around like a gypsy? Robert, what's going on in your home?" So let's just get out of the tree, alright pal?

BOBBY JR.: No.

ROBERT: No?

BOBBY JR.: No.

ROBERT: No?

BOBBY JR.: No.

ROBERT: No.

> (Beat)

That's it. You asked for it. I'm coming up.

> (Robert attempts to climb the tree a few times. He has no luck.)

ROBERT: How in the hell did you do this . . . do you have claws or something?

BOBBY JR.: You're just too fat.

ROBERT: Hey. I may have put on a few pounds over the last couple of months, but I am not fat.

BOBBY JR.: That's what Autumn said to me at school on Friday. She said, "Your dad's getting fat. He must still be depressed."

ROBERT: Depressed? Me? Depressed? Well, I can tell you one thing. Autumn is destined to work middle management for the rest of her life, so I advise you not to listen to anything she has to say. And what kind of name is that anyway? Autumn. What gives some girl named Autumn the right to call me fat and depressed . . .

> (Robert looks at his stomach and then looks at his watch.)

ROBERT: OK, Bobby. No more fooling around here. Let's go.

BOBBY JR.: No.

ROBERT: No?

BOBBY JR.: No.

ROBERT: No. Unbelievable.

(Robert sits on the ground, somewhat defeated.)

ROBERT: We'll just stay here then, until you decide to come down. You've made your point, Bobby. What I say doesn't matter. Your mother, though . . . she's going to be very upset about this. Grandpa and Nana are probably looking at their menus right now and saying to each other, "Oh my, I hope there hasn't been a terrible car accident — again. It's probably Robert's fault — again." God.

(A long moment.)

BOBBY JR.: Is Autumn right?

ROBERT: Look. I told you, I'm not fat. It's called middle-aged. You'll see in about thirty years.

BOBBY JR.: I mean, are you depressed?

ROBERT: What difference does it make? I get up in the morning, right? I feed you breakfast, send you off to school, go to work, come home, feed you dinner, help you with your homework, put you to bed, watch TV and stuff my face with food and worry about you and eventually, around 3 or 4 AM, I fall asleep. Or at least I think I fall asleep. But I get up the next morning, don't I? And I do it all again. Is that depressed? I don't know. I don't know.

BOBBY JR.: Autumn says it's not normal to talk about Mom the way you do.

(Robert stands up.)

ROBERT: *Again* with this girl . . . What does Autumn know about normal? But more importantly, Bobby, how does she know enough about my behaviors to determine whether or not they're normal?

BOBBY JR.: Autumn likes Mom's scarves. She says they're beautiful.

ROBERT: OK, sure. They are beautiful. But that's not answering my question . . .

BOBBY JR.: She is the only one who talks to me at school. Everyone else makes fun of me, OK?

(A moment.)

ROBERT: I didn't know that. Why don't I know this? Why didn't you tell me?

BOBBY JR.: I'm telling you now, OK? Me and Autumn, we're best friends.

ROBERT: Ohhhh.

(Beat)

So that means you talk to Autumn about me, right?

BOBBY JR.: Yeah. Sometimes.

ROBERT: Sometimes. I see.

BOBBY JR.: I didn't call you fat or anything.

ROBERT: Well that's good to hear.

BOBBY JR.: It's just that sometimes you do you this thing.

ROBERT: Thing? I do this thing? What thing?

BOBBY JR.: You do this thing where you talk about Mom like she can still do stuff. Like, you say Mom is going to be mad or happy or that Mom will be upset because we're going to be late for brunch. But she can't be upset. Not anymore she can't.

(Beat.)

Is that normal?

(A moment.)

ROBERT: No. I guess that isn't normal. Is it?

(There is a long silence. Robert eventually looks at his watch.)

ROBERT: You're not coming down, are you?

BOBBY JR.: No.

ROBERT: No. Well then. I'm going to call the restaurant and tell your grandparents that we have to reschedule brunch for some other Sunday.

(Robert goes to leave, then turns around.)

ROBERT: Bobby?

BOBBY JR.: Yeah?

ROBERT: What does Autumn say about you?

BOBBY JR.: What do you mean?

ROBERT: What does she have to say about you wearing Mom's scarves?

BOBBY JR.: Nothing.

ROBERT: Nothing?

BOBBY JR.: I told Autumn why I wear them.

ROBERT: Why? I mean, why do you wear her scarves?

BOBBY JR.: Because they still smell like her.

ROBERT: Oh.

BOBBY JR.: Hey Dad?

ROBERT: Yeah?

BOBBY JR.: You want to smell one?

ROBERT: Sure.

(One scarf floats down and then another and another until it's raining scarves on Robert. Eventually about fifteen scarves settle to the ground. Robert picks one up and smells. Then he gathers a few more in his hands and breathes them in. Blackout.)

END OF PLAY

THE STREAK

GARY RICHARDS

CHARACTERS
    JOE, fifties
    LOU, thirties

SETTING
    A Detroit hotel room

• • •

*The set: a Detroit hotel room. The time: May 2, 1939. Afternoon. As the lights
come up, the stage is bare. On a tray stand is a room service tray, the tins still
covering the hot food. There is a knock on the door. Joe, a stocky gray-haired
man in his fifties, enters from the bathroom wiping the excess shaving cream
off his face with a towel.*

JOE: Coming, coming . . .
    *(Joe walks over to the door and opens it. Standing in the hallway is Lou, a
    handsome man in his mid-thirties.)*
    Hey, Lou, what are you doing here?
LOU: Can I have a minute of your time?
JOE: Of course, of course. Come in, please. I just got done shaving. I always
    shave before a game. I need to feel clean, ready, fresh. Know what I mean?
    Some managers go for that unshaven slovenly look. Not me. I'm a busi-
    nessman. My three-piece suit just happens to be a baseball uniform, that's
    all. Hey, I just got room service delivered. I'm always so ravenous before
    a game. Come to think of it, I'm always ravenous after a game, too. Sit.
    Have a bite with me.
LOU: No thanks.
JOE: C'mon. A nibble.
LOU: Can I speak to you for a minute?
JOE: Of course, of course. Make yourself comfortable. Do you mind if I eat?
LOU: No. Please. Go ahead.
JOE: What's the matter, you and the Babe butting heads?
LOU: No. He doesn't bother me.
JOE: You just let me know if he does. What the hell would that beached whale
    do without baseball? Then again, what would any of us do without base-
    ball? This . . . this game that grown men play. Someone throws a ball,
    someone tries to hit it and run around and touch these things called
    "bases." *(Joe lifts a tin off the lunch tray.)* Geeze!! I told them "mashed,"

not "baked." I can't believe it! I'm telling you, Lou, you can't get good help these days. You sure you don't want any?

LOU: No, thanks. Joe, it's . . .

JOE: And look it this. No ketchup! How the hell am I supposed to eat steak without ketchup?! What's the world coming to, Lou? Tell me.

LOU: I don't know, Joe.

JOE: Now I'm going to have to go down to housekeeping and ring somebody's neck. Do think I want to go down to housekeeping and kick some ass? No. I don't. But now I feel I don't have a choice. Their choice was to screw up my room service. My choice is to take somebody's head off. It's all about choice. Right Lou? *(Joe begins to eat.)*

JOE: C'mon, have a bite. You're looking a little thin these days.

LOU: No, thank you. Joe, this is really hard for me to say.

JOE: Say it. Say what's on your mind.

LOU: Well, I've been thinking.

JOE: That's good. That's good. It shows you're alive. But don't do it too much. Baseball is mostly about instinct. Sometimes you've got to leave your brain out of it.

LOU: Joe, I've come to the . . .

JOE: This steak is overdone, dammit! I said I wanted it medium rare! I specifically said "medium rare with a side order of mashed." Does that sound like "well done with a side of baked?" No. It doesn't. It's like missing a sign on the base path. There's no room for that kind of crap, is there, Lou? You and I both know this!

LOU: No, sir. No room at all. Joe?

JOE: So. Tell me. How are doing, Lou?

LOU: That's what I came to talk about.

JOE: Listen, if it's about your slump, don't worry about it. I'm not worried about it. Neither should you. Everything works itself out.

LOU: No, it's . . .

JOE: I've seen you work yourself out of slumps. That's the only thing you could do. It's early in the season. The weather has been . . .

LOU: No, it's not the weather. It's . . .

JOE: Listen to me. Be more patient. That's the key. Patience. Even in baseball, patience is a virtue. We've talked about this. So they give me a baked potato. Do they bother to put in sour cream? No. How the hell am I going to eat a baked potato without smothering it in sour cream?

LOU: I don't know, Joe.

JOE: Yes, sir. Patience. I've been watching you. You're usually a lot more patient up at the plate. Somehow, for some reason, these days you seem . . .

LOU: It's my concentration.

JOE: I can see that. Tell me. What's going on? You're not watching the ball come out of the pitcher's hand like you usually do. I mean, that's what separates the stars from the rest of the players. The ability to focus on the moment the pitcher releases the ball. You're one of the best. But don't worry. That concentration, that focus will come back to you. It's elusive. Like a fly ball in the sun.

LOU: It's not only my hitting, Joe. My fielding has been atrocious.

JOE: Lou, Lou, Lou, a couple of bad hops, a couple of errors, a terrible infield, a pebble in the dirt. Big deal. These things happen. Last night I complained about the infield to the idiot head umpire. He says to me, "What do you want me to do, Joe, get my lawnmower and rake? I was going to play the game under protest, but after we took a four-run lead in the fourth, I figured what the heck. At least these vegetables are good. How's the wife?

LOU: She's . . . fine.

JOE: Any trouble at home?

LOU: No.

JOE: Listen, if it's about your contract, I told . . .

LOU: It's not about my contract.

JOE: Listen, your hitting, your fielding, it's a long season, Lou. You know that better than anyone. It's May. We just got started.

LOU: I was horrible at the end of last year as well.

JOE: Were you?

LOU: You know I was. *(Lou turns to Joe.)* Joe?

JOE: Yeah?

LOU: It's over.

JOE: What?

LOU: The streak. It's over.

JOE: What are you talking about?

LOU: I'm not going to be in the lineup tonight.

JOE: What?

LOU: You're not going to pencil me into the lineup for tonight's game.

JOE: But . . . but . . .

LOU: I can't play tonight. At this point, I'm the only one that can do it so . . . I'm benching myself.

JOE: You're benching yourself?

LOU: Yes.

JOE: Why?

LOU: I . . . I'm not feeling well.

JOE: You're . . . you're . . . *(Pause.)* I'll tell you what we'll do. We can do what we've done a couple of times in the past. I'll put you in the lineup, you'll lead off the top of the first, you'll get your at bat, I'll put in a sub. No big deal. Remember the game against . . .

LOU: No, Joe. I can't play tonight.

JOE: I'll tell you what I'll do. I'll call the general manager. The forecast is for rain. He can call off the game on the account of rain. We've done that before.

LOU: Joe, there's not a cloud in the sky.

JOE: Same as last time! Doesn't matter! *(Pause.)* I'll tell you what we'll do. We could . . .

LOU: Mr. McCarthey, stop it!

JOE: Don't tell me to stop it! I'll be damned if I'm going to go down in history as the manager who benched the "Iron Horse!" "Oh, there goes Joe McCarthey, the idiot who made Lou Gehrig break his consecutive game streak!" No way! Don't do this to me!

LOU: I have four lousy singles in seven games!

JOE: It's a slump! It's a slump! It's called a slump, for chrissake! Everyone goes through slumps. You've got to play your way out of it, that's all. That's the only way!

LOU: I'm not seeing the ball, Joe! I'm not seeing the ball!

JOE: Lou . . .

LOU: I'm having trouble getting comfortable in the batter's box.

JOE: But, Lou, I . . .

LOU: I have no strength in my legs. My arms feel weak, like toothpicks.

JOE: That's because . . .

LOU: The bat feels heavy in my hands.

JOE: Switch to a lighter . . .

LOU: I'm having trouble running out ground balls. I'm having trouble making the stretch at first base!

JOE: Don't do this to me!

LOU: This has nothing to do with you! It has to do with me! It has to do with the fans who pay their hard earned money to watch men at the top of their game. They deserve that! And I'm not giving it to them, Joe. I'm not at the top of my game. And I haven't been for a while.

JOE: You not "at the top" is still better than . . .

LOU: Joe, I know what I feel. And I feel it in my guts. Don't you think it torments me to break the streak? It does. But it torments me even more to know that I'm standing in the batter's box and I'm a detriment to the team. I'm not going to let myself be a detriment to this great team! I can't do it! That's not who I am! I am no longer capable of playing up to the standards that . . .

JOE: Wait, wait, wait! Whose standards?

LOU: My standards! My standards! My standards!

(A beat. Joe paces the room.)

JOE: You realize what you're asking me to do?

LOU: Yes. I do. A while back my wife wanted me to stop at 1,999. She always thought that people would remember that figure. But I kept going. I've played with broken fingers, broken toes, back spasms, viruses, stomachaches, headaches, all sorts of ailments. Remember that exhibition game when I was hit on the head? I wasn't afraid for my life. I was afraid the streak would die. So I played the next day with a bump on my head the size of Wyoming.

JOE: And you hit three triples that day until the game was rained out.

LOU: I always thought the fans wanted me to continue. That the writers and the newspapers wanted me to continue. So I did. When I broke Everett Scott's record, and the Babe said that the "Iron Man stuff was a bunch of baloney," I became obsessed. As long as I felt I was not damaging the team's chances to win, I played. *(Pause.)* Joe?

JOE: Yeah?

LOU: Look at me.

(Joe turns and faces Lou.)

I'm damaging the team's chances to win.

JOE: But . . .

LOU: No "buts," Joe. *(Pause.)* It's over. Something . . .

JOE: What?

LOU: . . . something is wrong.

JOE: What?

LOU: *(Pause.)* I don't know, Joe. I don't know. All I know is that something is wrong.

JOE: *(Pause.)* I can't talk you out of it?

LOU: No.

JOE: *(Pause.)* Very well. It's your call. Always has been. Can I say something to the team?

LOU: Let them find out when they look at the lineup card.

JOE: The press?

LOU: They'll find out soon afterwards. I'll be ready for them.

(A long beat.)

JOE: I'm sorry.

LOU: Don't be. I'm the luckiest guy in the world.

(Lou goes to the door.)

JOE: Lou? You set a record that will never be broken.

LOU: *(Pause.)* You never know.

JOE: Hey, Lou, it's been an honor.

LOU: Me too.

JOE: Lou, I . . . I . . .

LOU: What is it, Joe?

JOE: I love you.

LOU: Me too.

(Joe goes to Lou and embraces him tightly. A beat. Lou nods, opens the door, and exits Joe walks over to the tray stand. He sits and begins to cut his steak. He suddenly throws down his utensils. He stands. He walks over to the window. He stares out. The lights fade to black.)

END OF PLAY

PLAYS FOR
TWO WOMEN

THE DRESS REHEARSAL

Marisa Smith

Originally produced by The Parish Players of Thetford Hill,
Vermont, at the Eclipse Grange Theater on February 9 to 11,
2007. Cast: Dorothy — Deborah Solomon;
Marti — Suzanne Schon.

CHARACTERS

DOROTHY, woman in her sixties
MARTI (MARTHA), her daughter, in her thirties

SETTING

The present somewhere in the Northeast

•   •   •

The present day. Family room. Two upholstered chairs flank a round table covered with a floor-length tablecloth and it is piled with reading material. There are newspapers, books, and magazines on the floor. Loud funeral music is playing on a small Bose system on the table. There is a small side table with a decanter and two sherry glasses. Dorothy is asleep in one of the chairs, People *magazine is open on her chest. She's dressed nicely, in slacks and a sweater, something she probably bought at Talbots. Marti opens the back door and enters upstage of Dorothy.*

MARTI: Mom? Mother, it's me. *(Marti walks into the room and sees Dorothy asleep in the chair. She looks around at the mess, turns off the music. She begins to straighten the mess, and then kneels in front of Dorothy and gently touches her. Dorothy suddenly awakens.)*

DOROTHY: *(Yells.)* Ahhhhhhh!

MARTI: *(Yells.)* Ahhhhhhh!

DOROTHY AND MARTI: *(They yell together.)* Ahhhhhh!

MARTI: I'm sorry, the door was open.

DOROTHY: Oh, honey, I didn't hear you come in. *(Her hand is on her heart.)* My heart got a little work out!

MARTI: You wanted me for lunch today?

DOROTHY: I want you for lunch every day honey.

MARTI: But you said *today*, right?

DOROTHY: I've just been reading about that horrible Bridget Spears. What a little whore. She looks like one of those check-out girls at Price Chopper if you ask me. And that poor Nancy Allen, you remember that cute actress who was in *Blow Up?*— some newspaper reported that she was *dead* and she had to go on national TV to prove that she was still *alive*, imagine!

MARTI: *Blow* Out. It was *Blow* Out.

DOROTHY: Oh, your hair. Oh, I love your hair. Is it blonder? I love it blonde. Or is it darker now?

MARTI: I'm thinking of going back to my natural color.

DOROTHY: Oh . . . I see.

MARTI: People take brunettes more seriously.

DOROTHY: But, you look *younger*, honey, when you're blonde. Not that you look *old* —

MARTI: Yeah, Ma, I know you like it blonde.

DOROTHY: You don't have to get *nasty* about it. *(Changing the subject.)* Don't look at my piles. I'm organizing everything, a total *purge.* Harry whatshisface, Hennessy or Heineken, I can never remember — you know, Dad's nephew from Troy — he's coming this weekend. You remember the one with all the wives that kept dying — fat, fatter, and fattest. *(She laughs heartily at her own joke.)* Oh, I'm horrible; God's going to strike me down and just when I went back to the church. *(Pause.)* How's Irving? I called yesterday but he probably forgot to tell you, you know how men are. *(Changing the subject again.)* Did you just do the New Year's holiday or the atoning one? How do you keep them straight, they're so many! I'm making us some sherry, let's live a little. *(Hands her a glass of sherry.)*

MARTI: It's Rosh Hashanah and Yom Kippur Mother, it's not that hard. *(Drinks her sherry.)* Harry's coming this weekend?

DOROTHY: I think that's what your father said. Maybe it's next weekend.

MARTI: 'Cause I was hoping you could take Jason for the weekend. Irv and I have plans to go into the city for our anniversary and Jase was supposed to stay at Jeremy's but he got sick—

DOROTHY: Well, of course we'd love to have him but it might be a little crowded with Harry and whatshername. We'll manage. If Jason doesn't mind the couch —

MARTI: No, it's OK. I'll see if he can go to Tucker's.

DOROTHY: What, you won't let me have my own grandson? I have to beg?

MARTI: I didn't say that Mother.

DOROTHY: Have I ever said no to you, have I?

MARTI: Mother —

DOROTHY: And how is the blinking? Is he still blinking?

MARTI: Please don't bother him about the blinking. The doctor said it's a phase —

DOROTHY: You're afraid I'll bring up the blinking? That's why you don't want me to have him?

MARTI: No, you said it would be crowded.

DOROTHY: Maybe it's time I did said no to you.

MARTI: *Fine*, say no, it's *fine.*

DOROTHY: Well, I just might. I have to see when the Herpes are coming and if they're bringing their RV or not.

MARTI: It's the *Hennikers* Mother. Harry and Darlene Henniker, you've known them for over thirty years!

DOROTHY: Well, I hope you're hungry. I'm making us a fabulous lunch. Pasta in a bag. You just throw it in a saucepan with water and it heats up in a second, look here it is. *(Hands her the bag.)*

MARTI: *(Reading the label.)* Ma, there's enough sodium in here to kill you.

DOROTHY: You're not going to start are you? Can't we just have a nice time?

MARTI: Fine.

DOROTHY: That reminds me, I saw *him* on *LA Law* last night, just a small part but . . .

MARTI: It's a record Ma; it only took you two minutes and thirty seconds to bring up Scott.

DOROTHY: He sent me a card for my birthday. With llamas on it.

MARTI: I know, you told me.

DOROTHY: I still can't believe it — a beautiful girl like you.

MARTI: Ma, it's been fifteen years.

DOROTHY: I know, I know, it's just one of life's little mysteries.

MARTI: He's gay Mother, there's nothing mysterious about it. A fairy. Queer. Light in the loafers. Friend of Dorothy, ha, ha, no pun intended. *(Suddenly searches for cigarettes in her purse.)*

DOROTHY: OK, OK don't rub it in. I *get* it, Judy Garland. You think your mother is so stupid. I just thought you could turn him around. I mean look what Elizabeth Taylor did for Montgomery Clift —

MARTI: *(Yelling.)* She did nothing for him! He drove himself into a telephone pole and he drank himself to death! *(Starts to light her cigarette.)*

DOROTHY: THIS IS A NO SMOKING ZONE. I'm not up to this today, Martha. I don't want to scare you but I may have to have another kidney scan.

MARTI: There you go.

DOROTHY: What?

MARTI: The kidneys. Whenever you want to change the subject you bring out those ol' kidneys.

DOROTHY: I'm not trying to change the subject.

MARTI: You are too!

DOROTHY: Stop picking on me!

MARTI: I am not!

DOROTHY: Yes you are!

MARTI: You are so thin-skinned!

DOROTHY: There you go again!

MARTI: This is so unbelievably STUPID!

DOROTHY: It's not that time of the month is it? I've started to put a big red X on my calendar so I try not to take you so personally.

MARTI: No, Mother, I'm not PMSing. You said you had something to chat with me about.

DOROTHY: More sherry?

MARTI: MO-THER! Why did you ask me here, what's the deal, what's going on?

DOROTHY: *(Pours more.)* Well, I was watching the History Channel and they were doing a documentary about Charles the Fifth, you know—

MARTI: *(Impatiently.)* Yes, I know The Holy Roman Emperor one.

DOROTHY: Son of Philip the Handsome . . . and Joanna the Mad.

MARTI: I'm not touching that one.

DOROTHY: Anyway, it turns out that he was odd — all those old Kings were — but he did do this one thing that I thought was very interesting.

MARTI: Interesting?

DOROTHY: Apparently, before he actually died, he, well, he staged a *dress rehearsal* of his funeral.

MARTI: A dress rehearsal. Open or closed casket?

DOROTHY: Oh, I don't know honey. The point is, he was able to see how it would be when he did die.

MARTI: Novel.

DOROTHY: And he got to hear the eulogies and the music and I was thinking . . . what a great idea!

MARTI: You're joking.

DOROTHY: I mean, why not? People die every day and they never get to know what their friends thought and how much they meant to everyone. It's such a shame. I'm going to be completely honest here —

MARTI: Oh, no—

DOROTHY: I don't want one of those little obits in the *Gazette*. I'm not going to be Miss Humble. I want *you* to write it and mention every one of my accomplishments! The Garden Club, you know I was the General of the Tulip Brigade, the Dog Biscuit Bake-Off, we raised over five thousand dollars for the Pet Cemetery, Planned Parenthood — it was my idea to have a diaphragm mobile and that was a *huge* success . . .

MARTI: You really should write it yourself, Mom.

DOROTHY: I want to do more than that; I want to do what Charles the Fifth did. I want a dress rehearsal.

MARTI: Of your own funeral — you want a dress rehearsal of your funeral? How exactly would that work, Mother?

DOROTHY: I've thought that whole thing through.

MARTI: *(Under her breath.)* That's a first.

DOROTHY: And I want you to be the "director." It will be just like one of the plays you do at the high school.

MARTI: What? You want me to be in charge, are you nuts!

DOROTHY: There will come a time — you have to face this honey — when it will become clear that I don't have much time left. You can confer with Dr. Benson — oh that dear, wonderful man — and before I lapse into a coma or something — the whole point is that I have to be compus mentis — you'll announce that I've passed and start planning the funeral.

MARTI: Mother, you can't do that! There's like a death certificate to sign and a doctor has to pronounce you dead or something —

DOROTHY: Those are just details honey, they can all be worked out. Maybe Dr. B will go along with this — this is my last wish after all and he's been my physician for over thirty years — he's probably seen me naked more than your father has —

MARTI: Please! Not a good image, Mother . . .

DOROTHY: Let me sketch out the broad outline. So, we announce my death, well, *you* announce it. It's in the paper, I'll choose the photo. Realistic, not a young shot, *refined.* I'll give you a list of people that I want to talk. I'll pick the music, the flowers, nothing white, NO carnations, I want bold, beautiful blooms, I want this to be a celebration of my life! A slide show might be nice, no fat pictures obviously, and you have my permission to use the nude ones Dad took on our honeymoon — they are really art shots. Yes, a wall of photos at the reception not the church —

MARTI: Jesus God. St. Stephen's?

DOROTHY: Of course, with that sweet Father Patrick officiating. He loves me. They love it when a sheep returns.

MARTI: But you can't ask a priest to preside over a phony funeral Mother, he'd never do it!

DOROTHY: Never say never. They're renovating the rectory.

MARTI: You'd pay him off?

DOROTHY: This is my last wish Marti. After this the movie is over! OK, I'm in the casket.

MARTI: You're in the casket?

DOROTHY: It has air holes and *I'm* not claustrophobic in the *least* as you know.

MARTI: *(Sarcastic.)* Well, that's good.

DOROTHY: That's the beauty of this whole plan, no one knows I'm there but I am! I'm listening to the speeches and Father Patrick and the organ plays, maybe the choir is there, they sound like angels, and it's giving me real closure, I feel I can die happy, I feel like I've made a contribution —

MARTI: Mother, it's so unbelievably deceitful! You're asking me to lie to Jason, to all your friends —

DOROTHY: You can't grant your mother her very last wish, the mother who never said no to you? Did I, did I ever say no?

MARTI: Jesus, enough with the NO already — you're like a dog with a bone. This crazy plan could even be illegal!

DOROTHY: If you loved me you'd want me to be happy. Don't you love me Marti?

MARTI: It doesn't have anything do to with love.

DOROTHY: It has everything to do with love! I've done so much for you! You know, I've wracked my brain and I can't think of one thing, not one thing that I've ever asked of you, ever. Not one! I let you quit piano —

MARTI: I broke my hand!

DOROTHY: — you went to the college of your choice —

MARTI: You begged me to go to Mt. Holyoke!

DOROTHY: You married who you wanted . . . both times.

MARTI: You fainted in the synagogue!

DOROTHY: I never pressured you for more grandchildren, which I would have loved —

MARTI: *You* only had one!

DOROTHY: You should have learned from my mistake! You could have adopted.

MARTI: *You* could have adopted!

DOROTHY: Well, your *father* didn't want to!

MARTI: *I* didn't want to!

DOROTHY: How did I raise such a selfish girl!

MARTI: I almost died giving birth to Jason!

DOROTHY: No one dies in childbirth anymore. That's an exaggeration! Irving always says that!

MARTI: I was bleeding to death!

DOROTHY: You were not!

MARTI: I was too! Not that you cared.

DOROTHY: Of course I care. I care more than anyone! You were never dying, never! Don't say that!

MARTI: All the sympathy you would have had if I died, sympathy for life, you could have dined out on it forever!

DOROTHY: That's a horrible thing to say, horrible!

MARTI: You even lie to yourself, it's unbelievable. You are totally reality averse!

DOROTHY: You used to be sweet and good and ever since you married Irving, you think he's so perfect, well he's not, he's not —

MARTI: You don't care if I'm happy! You still want me married to your precious
Scott! God help us if that asshole become famous, you'll never let me forget it for one second — I'll have to move to Anarctica. Fucking Scott —
he always sucked up to you, it made me sick!

DOROTHY: Scott loved me, he treated me with respect!

MARTI: He thought you were an idiot!

DOROTHY: You just couldn't keep him and you're taking it out on me! What's
wrong with you!

MARTI: You don't know where you end and I begin and you keep punishing
me for not being what *you* want! *(Picks up* People *magazine.)* You wor-
ship at the altar of *PEOPLE* MAGAZINE! I tell my friends that if I were
a serial murderer and killed a thousand people and my face were on this
cover you'd buy a million copies and hand them out to everyone you
know!

DOROTHY: You are *killing* me! You never talk like this! This is a nightmare! I'm
putting on the pasta! *(Dorothy exits.)*

MARTI: *(Marti throws herself in a chair, shaken by her outburst, slams* People *down.
Totally unraveled, she pulls cigarettes and matches out of her purse and lights
one. Dorothy enters carrying a wine bottle, and stares at Marti who continues to smoke.)*

DOROTHY: Can you open this? My hands you know, the arthritis.

MARTI: *(Looks at bottle.)* It's a screw top . . .

DOROTHY: I can't do it. *(Marti twists off the top and hands it back to Dorothy.)*

DOROTHY: *(Petulantly.)* Thank you. Lunch will be ready in five minutes. I'm
not hungry but I hope that *you'll* eat something —

MARTI: *(Takes a long look at her MOTHER.)* You know Ma, the dress rehearsal thing, I mean its loony, but if you're really serious —

DOROTHY: Oh, honey! Marti!

MARTI: At least we can *explore* it.

DOROTHY: Thank you sweetie. Oh, and when I was in the kitchen I checked
the calendar and the "Hennikers" aren't coming for two weekends. I *insist*
on having Jason this weekend, you and Irving go into the city. Have fun!

MARTI: Great, thanks. *(Picks up magazine from one of the piles.)* Casket Quar-
terly? Who knew?

DOROTHY: Maybe this week we could go to the funeral home — Ward's, not
Dalessi's, they're so tacky. And those things you said —

MARTI: Oh, God, I think I *am* getting my period.

DOROTHY: You must be.

DOROTHY: *(Picking up cigarettes.)* May I have one?

MARTI: You don't smoke.

DOROTHY: On occasion.

MARTI: Noo. *(Lights Dorothy's cigarette with her cigarette.)*

DOROTHY: *(Exhaling.)* Honey, there a lot of things about your old mother that you don't know. *(They smoke together as the lights fade to black.)*

END OF PLAY

HANGING ON

CLAUDIA HAAS

Original Production: American Stage Theatre Company, St. Petersburg, Florida, *10X10 Play Festival*, January 25, 26, 29, February 1, 2, 2007. Cast: Jennifer — Meg Heimstead; Melanie — Nevada Caldwell. Director: Bob Devin Jones. Curator of Festival: T. Scott Wooten. Second Production: Northfield Arts Guild, April 28, 2007. Cast: Jennifer — Donna Beard; Melanie — Elana Gravitz. Director: Jan Arford.

CHARACTERS

JENNIFER, female, late twenties, overwhelmed writer looking for normal, mundane, health insurance

MELANIE, female, late twenties, actress just tasting a bit of success and hanging on

SETTING

A cramped and shabby but eclectic studio apartment; all one needs to be visible is a table and a chair or two with books and papers lying around. It is possible to do this with no furniture.

It is early in the morning in the spring.

SYNOPSIS

Overwhelmed by what it takes to succeed in a competitive world, Jennifer has decided to chuck it all in while Melanie persuades her to "hang on."

∙ ∙ ∙

AT RISE we are in a cramped, one-bedroom apartment. Clutter abounds. One entrance leads to a small kitchenette and another to the bedroom and bath. Jennifer stumbles from her bedroom in her morning attire (sweats) carrying a cup of coffee and a many loose papers. From the kitchen, Melanie is in the kitchen. It is a cold spring, weekday morning at about 6:30 AM. Jennifer puts her coffee down and methodically starts to rip her papers.

MELANIE: *(From offstage.)* Coffee?

JENNIFER: *(Still ripping papers.)* Have it, already. Thanks.

MELANIE: I have a surprise! Don't go anywhere.

JENNIFER: Where would I go?

MELANIE: *(Appearing holding a cake with ten candles.)* Voila!

JENNIFER: What's that?

MELANIE: I know it's early — but really, the answer should be obvious.

JENNIFER: It's a cake!

MELANIE: Oh, you are good.

JENNIFER: We don't normally eat cake at dawn. You never eat cake.

MELANIE: Well, it's sugarless of course. And made with whole wheat flour and some bran. But today is the day, remember? The day we chucked our teaching jobs and moved to the big city to pursue our dreams. I thought we should celebrate. You've been a bit down lately and I thought this would perk you up.

JENNIFER: You thought a sugarless cake made with whole wheat flour and some bran would bring me cheer? Is there chocolate in it?

MELANIE: Figs and applesauce. Very healthy.

JENNIFER: But not comforting.

MELANIE: I'm on Broadway now. I have to watch my weight.

JENNIFER: You walk on at the very end of the play and need to keep your waitress job to pay the bills.

MELANIE: JEN!

JENNIFER: I'm sorry, Mel. I haven't forgotten what day it is. And it's been ten years. Do you realize that? Ten years!

MELANIE: Note the number of candles on the cake.

JENNIFER: Well, I decided to do my own celebration. In honor of the day, I am taking every rejection letter and tearing it apart.

MELANIE: That's great! Thinking positive! I never understood why you kept those things around anyway.

JENNIFER: Initially, it was to throw the letters back into the faces of every theater who turned me down. After I made it, of course. Well, I'm done. Do you remember what my New Year's resolution was?

MELANIE: To get a New York production. That's always your New Years resolution.

JENNIFER: No, Mel. Not this time. This time I was resolved to get health insurance. Do you realize we are now in our thirties and don't have health insurance?

MELANIE: Well, I have some — 'cause of the play. But I don't think about it. I just resolve to stay healthy.

JENNIFER: I'm changing, Mel. The artistic fever is going and I now crave health insurance. And 401(k)s.

MELANIE: What?

JENNIFER: 401 — never mind. This is it! I've piled up the manuscripts in the back. They're being recycled today. I'm tearing up every rejection letter, every offer to submit, every online playwriting course — it's all going. I'm cleansing!

MELANIE: Have a piece of cake. It'll help you . . . cleanse.

JENNIFER: Figs and bran? Really Mel, what were you thinking?

MELANIE: *(Picking up a torn piece of paper.)* Jen! These rejections are very nice. They should keep you going.

(Reading.)

"You have a sparkling wit that shines like a glass of champagne." That's nice, Jen!

JENNIFER: Read on.

MELANIE: "Unfortunately when we do champagne comedies, we produce Noel Coward."

JENNIFER: *(Handing her a piece of paper.)* Look at this.

MELANIE: "The play is exceedingly well-crafted. We enjoyed the twists and turns along the way and the surprise ending truly was inspirational." Jennifer! What do you have to be depressed about? These are the loveliest rejection letters!

JENNIFER: *(Retrieving the paper.)* "However, your cast size is daunting and your set is likely to be expensive."

MELANIE: OK — so reduce the cast size.

JENNIFER: There are three people in the cast!

MELANIE: Cut down on your set requirements.

JENNIFER: It's a unit set! A shabby living room! What do they want? An alleyway? A street? If they want that, they might as well just do *Waiting for Godot* over and over again. Wait! They can't. It requires four people. The cast is too large!

MELANIE: What do they always say, "Write about what you know."

JENNIFER: I did! The play is about three actresses living in a shabby one-bedroom apartment.

MELANIE: It's about — what?

JENNIFER: It's — you know about lives of struggling artists . . . sort of . . .

MELANIE: It isn't about us, is it?

JENNIFER: NO! Well — it's about me, really. I mean if I know anything, I know me!

MELANIE: *(Getting a bit worried here.)* Am I in it?

JENNIFER: Well . . . sort of — but not really. Disguised. And nice. Really nice.

MELANIE: I need to read it.

JENNIFER: NO! I mean, I need to edit — oh, who am I kidding? I'm dumping it. It's over. The dreaming. The work. The depressions. I'm done. I want forty hours a week with benefits.

MELANIE: Jennifer — it's so . . .

JENNIFER: Mundane. I know. My pursuit of art has left me craving the mundane! I yearn for the ordinary! Not, "Although we cannot use you this time, we encourage you to submit some more."

MELANIE: So, you keep submitting until they can use you! They're telling you to keep writing.

JENNIFER: I can go back home, update my teaching skills and work, Melanie! One job. Not three.

MELANIE: But these rejection letter — they're filled with hope.

JENNIFER: That's the worst thing they've done. You know how you are always saying, "I wish they wouldn't tell me how wonderful I am after an audition. That just makes me sit by the phone expecting them to call. It would be more professional if they would just say, NEXT!"

MELANIE: That's different.

JENNIFER: How is it different? Positive rejection letters do the same to me. They make me write another play and I get the same old "It's quite entertaining but not what we can use at the moment." I have no idea what they can use —

MELANIE: Stop it! You don't write what "they" can use. You write what's in your heart. What comes from you — and then match it up with a theater who is looking for what you wrote. There are thousands of theaters out there. If you write it, they will produce.

JENNIFER: That's not what *you* do. You dress differently for each audition. You package yourself so that they can "use" you.

MELANIE: That's because producers have no imagination. I had better be what they want the moment I step in the doorway.

JENNIFER: So, you think producers of plays are highly imaginative? I mean, really — the theater can't envision a unit set! My "shabby living room" scenario is too expensive for them? Community theaters produce a set like that every six weeks!

MELANIE: OK — make a plan. If you're in the same place in one year —

JENNIFER: No! I have a plan. Sayonara. This is it! Iowa, here I come!

MELANIE: Jen, you cannot go back to Iowa. That's like living in a production of *Music Man*. It's not healthy.

JENNIFER: This is? Two single women in a one-bedroom apartment for ten years? TEN YEARS! That's a decade you know.

MELANIE: Yes, dear. I can measure time.

JENNIFER: And here we sit at 6:30 AM commemorating our success with a prune cake?

MELANIE: Figs and bran.

JENNIFER: People our age have lives, Melanie! They have mortgages . . . children . . . I don't know . . . cats! People our age know how to drive and they even own cars! They go to the dentist twice a year . . . .

MELANIE: Oh! The dentist! Let me pack my bags, return home and go to the dentist!

JENNIFER: There are straight men in Iowa!

MELANIE: OK. That's a plus. But you're still in Iowa.

JENNIFER: But living a life in which I move forward.

MELANIE: As do we. I am on Broadway now.

JENNIFER: I know — and —

MELANIE: — and I know I still have to waitress three lunches and a brunch to make ends meet . . . but it's more than I had last year. It's a credit and a fulfillment of a dream.

JENNIFER: I'm sorry. I shouldn't have made any cracks about your role. I'm happy for you.

MELANIE: And you had a play produced last month. Don't forget that.

JENNIFER: A one-page play. Let's not retire on my royalties yet.

MELANIE: It's a production. It's a start.

JENNIFER: I've had a hundred starts. False starts. False positives. I start and I start and I never get past GO. Buying Park Place is not in the dice. I'm tired of starting and not finishing. Starting and not ending. Always starting. Always living on these snippets of hope. I look around and after years of starting, I'm in exactly the same place as ten years ago.

MELANIE: As am I.

JENNIFER: No. You go to a Broadway theater every night. You put on costume and makeup —

MELANIE: And make my entrance just before the final blackout. God, I'm depressed.

JENNIFER: *(Cutting some cake.)* No! Stop it! You're out there doing it. Not obsessing over rejection letters. Come on, have a piece of cake.

MELANIE: I need chocolate. Figs. What was I thinking?

JENNIFER: It's not bad . . . you know . . . for healthy stuff. It could be worse. You could have added tofu. Have some.

(Jennifer cuts Melanie a piece.)

Oh! Wait! I have just the thing.

(Jennifer runs into the kitchen.)

MELANIE: What are you doing?

JENNIFER: It's a surprise! To go with your celebration.

(Jennifer appears with two champagne glasses and a half bottle of open champagne.)

Left over. From my little "One-Page-Play-Produced" little celebration. I have it on good authority it goes well with fig cake.

MELANIE: Flat champagne? At 6:40 AM?

JENNIFER: It's the only time to drink flat champagne. When you're depressed and half asleep.

MELANIE: I'm convinced.

(Jennifer pours some.)

You know, Jen — I've always wanted to ask you something.

JENNIFER: Now would be a good time. 'Cause by tomorrow I'll be enroute to Iowa.

MELANIE: You're a writer and I'm an actress.

JENNIFER: . . . was a writer, Mel. *Was* being the operative word.

MELANIE: Well, how come you never wrote anything for me? Did you think I wasn't a good enough actress to be in your plays?

JENNIFER: Melanie! Bite your tongue! I always thought you wouldn't want to be in my plays. That maybe you thought I didn't write well enough.

MELANIE: Are you nuts? I daydream about us collaborating. I was waiting for you to come up with an idea.

JENNIFER: You drop this on me, now? While I'm packing my bags for Iowa?

MELANIE: They're not packed yet. I was thinking — you know all those jobs I held —

JENNIFER: Which one? When you were the sandwich sign or when you polished shoes at the airport?

MELANIE: Don't forget the "Walking Pickle."

JENNIFER: No! The best was the singing telegrams. With the drum-playing monkey.

MELANIE: Well . . . I was thinking that those days could be fun to write about . . . and I would help you market it . . . I met this producer the other night who says these shows are really cheap to produce and actually earn income . . . .

JENNIFER: *(Very, very skeptical.)* Really?

MELANIE: Well, if you could just stick around till summer. I mean, nobody is going to hire a teacher right now with summer just ten weeks away . . . maybe we could write this thing.

JENNIFER: May-be.

MELANIE: For fun. Just for us, Jen. I mean, would you consider it?

JENNIFER: So, I just have to stick around till summer?

MELANIE: That's it. Just ten weeks. And then I'll look for a new roommate and throw you a Bon Voyage party. Would you do it? For me? It'll be fun. And maybe it will ignite your passion —

JENNIFER: No! Don't give me hope! I'll do it — for you. No more fresh starts.

MELANIE: No new starts, I promise. Let's toast.

(She lifts her champagne glass.)

To us! To our opening! "At rise we find an actress alone on stage dressed as a pickle."

JENNIFER: I'm telling you, you open with the monkey. It's a sight gag.

MELANIE: The pickle isn't?

JENNIFER: And then where do we go from there?

MELANIE: I don't know but I tell you what — we pass GO.
   (*They click their glasses as we fade to black.*)

END OF PLAY

MY BOYFRIEND'S WIFE

BARBARA LINDSAY

Original production: Theatre Workshop of Nantucket,
Nantucket Short Play Festival. Performed at Methodist Church,
2 Centre St., Nantucket, February 15–17, 22–24, 2007.
Director: Grace Noyes. Cast: Dodie — (first weekend) Susan
McGinnis, (second weekend) Annie Breeding;
Raina — Vicky Goss, (final performance) Pam Murphy.

CHARACTERS

    DODIE, a plain woman in her forties

    RAINA, a beautiful woman in her forties

SETTING

    A cemetery

TIME

    Late afternoon. Fall.

• • •

Lights up. Time: Late afternoon. Fall. Setting: A cemetery. At Rise: Dodie walks slowly past the gravesites reading the headstones. She carries a bouquet of roses and carnations. She comes to one headstone and stops.

(Pause.)

DODIE: There you are.

    (Pause.)

    I'm Dodie. I'm Allen's new girlfriend. Allen's girlfriend. Actually we're lovers. We're not living together yet or anything, but we spend a lot of time together. Mostly at his house. Your house. Anyway, I thought it was time you and I met.

    (Pause. She remembers the flowers and lays them down.)

    Allen said you used to like roses and carnations.

RAINA'S VOICE: Thank you. I still do.

DODIE: Me too.

    (Pause.)

    I've heard a lot about you. Seen your pictures. I almost feel like I know you. Almost. But I probably just have some idea about you. People don't go into detail much. You know, careful of my feelings and everything.

    (Pause.)

    Everybody misses you a lot.

RAINA'S VOICE: I miss them, too.

DODIE: Everybody misses you *a lot*. You were — you know, popular. Not popular, that's not the right word. Thought well of. Well-thought-of. You know. Close. Esteemed.

RAINA: Loved.

DODIE: Loved. You were very, very well loved. By everybody.

RAINA: Not by everybody.

DODIE: No. Only by the people who knew you.

(Long pause. Dodie finally looks at Raina.)

You're really beautiful.

RAINA: Thank you.

DODIE: I already knew that from your pictures, but . . . It's a little hard to take.

RAINA: I can imagine.

DODIE: No you can't.

(Long pause.)

Allen's doing great. You know, struggling sometimes. Sad sometimes. Kind of putting his life together again. Or maybe it's more like making a new life. I'm not sure.

RAINA: I'm glad to hear it.

DODIE: He is really terrific. God, he's a good guy. Something about him just goes right through me. Isn't he just . . . ? Oh man. You know.

RAINA: Yes he is.

DODIE: I just like him so much.

RAINA: He's very easy to love.

DODIE: Yeah, I guess I love him.

(Long pause.)

So.

(Pause.)

Anything you want to ask me? Or tell me?

RAINA: You came to me.

DODIE: That's true. I thought we ought to meet.

RAINA: And here we are.

DODIE: Right. You bet. Here we are.

(Pause.)

I don't exactly know how to say anything.

RAINA: That's all right. I have plenty of time.

DODIE: Yeah. Sort of nothing but, huh? So, what's it like, being dead and everything?

RAINA: Is that what you wanted to talk about?

DODIE: No. No. Just making conversation.

(Pause.)

Allen doesn't know I'm here, you know.

RAINA: Why not?

DODIE: I was afraid he might think it was a little intrusive, me wanting to pay you a visit. And it would be weird for me to be here with him. You know. This is a pretty private thing.

RAINA: Is it?

DODIE: Well yeah, it must be. You guys had a whole long life together that I'm not part of. And the whole watching you die thing. That was between you. That's very — intimate.

RAINA: Yes it is.

DODIE: It's intimate in a way . . . It's intimate in a way I don't know if he'll ever be with me.

RAINA: Don't worry. One of you is bound to die eventually.

DODIE: Yes, but I don't know if we'll be together when it happens. I don't know if . . . I don't know if I'll ever be . . .

RAINA: How long have you and he been together?

DODIE: Six months.

RAINA: How long were he and I married?

DODIE: Don't you know?

RAINA: Do you?

DODIE: Twenty years.

(Pause.)

OK, fine, but how long am I supposed to wait?

RAINA: Wait for what?

DODIE: To find out if he's ever going to love me. Or want to marry me. Or feel about me the way he does about you. Did. Does.

RAINA: I have no idea.

DODIE: Well come on. Don't you know things like that? Don't you get some sort of ghostly wisdom once you're off this earthly plane?

RAINA: I can't see the future, if that's what you're asking.

DODIE: What a rip-off. I thought that would be one of the perks of being dead.

RAINA: I can see what's in front of me more clearly.

DODIE: You mean me?

RAINA: In this moment.

DODIE: What do you see?

RAINA: You haven't said what you wanted to say.

DODIE: I don't know what I want to say. I don't know if I have the right to say anything. I don't know if I have the right to want anything.

RAINA: What a pickle.

DODIE: Yes, right there. That. Allen says that sometimes, too. First time I heard it, I knew it was one of those little shared phrases between the two of you. All sorts of things he says, I can tell, I can just tell that it's something you both used to say, like couple code, where you say it and then glance at each other, and it's all attached to memories and secrets and private jokes. Little pet names for things, ways of doing things, putting the coffee cups on the hooks just so. Who sleeps on which side of the bed. An earring on the windowsill. All the sentences his sisters start and then don't finish because they realize they're about to say your name, and I tell them, "It's all right, it's all right. It's all right to love her. It's all right to miss her," and they do, I know they do, they can't help themselves.

RAINA: And?

DODIE: "We." All these references to "we." "We did this, we went there, we were at the store one time. We used to, we used to . . . " And "we" always means you. It never means me.

RAINA: And?

DODIE: You're everywhere. You're everywhere. Sometimes I can't even remember who I am when I'm with him. I become just not-Raina. Not you.

RAINA: How long have you and Allen been together?

DODIE: I know, but —

RAINA: How long were he and I married?

DODIE: That's not the point.

RAINA: What point do you want to make?

DODIE: You have to let him go. It's time to let him go.

RAINA: No.

DODIE: What?

RAINA: No.

DODIE: Why not?

RAINA: Because he's not mine to let go of and he's not yours to hold on to. He doesn't belong to either one of us.

DODIE: Yes he does. He belongs to you. I can feel it, I can smell it on him. He loves you so much and I'm afraid he's never going to let me in.

RAINA: Boo hoo hoo.

DODIE: How do you think it feels to know that even if we get married, even if we're together for the next thirty years, when he dies, he's going to be buried right here, next to you.

RAINA: Buy the plot next to his.

DODIE: I'm going to be cremated.

RAINA: Then what on earth is the problem? What does it matter where we're buried? It's all just dead meat then.

DODIE: Because he's already chosen you for eternity. I'm never going to be the beloved. I'll never be the love of his life because he's already had her and it was you. I'll never be anything but second.

RAINA: And you don't like that.

DODIE: I can't stand it.

RAINA: That matters to you.

DODIE: More than anything.

RAINA: You get away from him.

DODIE: What? What do you mean?

RAINA: You get away and stay away. Don't you dare even come close to him. Get out of his heart, get out of his life, and get out of my house.

DODIE: What are you talking about?

RAINA: I mean it. If you try to use him that way, I will haunt you to the ends of the earth to the end of your days.

DODIE: I don't want to use him.

RAINA: Oh yes you do, and I won't have it.

DODIE: I just want to love him.

RAINA: No, you want to be loved by him. It's all about you, how you feel, how secure you get to be.

DODIE: That is not true.

RAINA: You want to be the beloved, win some kind of contest, own the biggest piece. I am on to you, you great big selfish baby. You think I'm all over your life with him now? Just wait until I come for you. My fingers will be on the back of your neck when you're with him. It's me you'll see when you look in his face. I'll be there with you when you're making love, my voice will be in your ear. "He doesn't love you, he'll never love you, he's thinking about me. He's mine, he's mine, he's mine."

DODIE: Oh my god. You're jealous.

RAINA: Jealous? Jealous? Why would I be jealous? Just because you're flesh and real and I'm a fading memory? Just because it's you he puts his hands on now? Just because I'll never be with him again? Just because you have years ahead of you to make a life with him?

To make a life? Jealous? Why would I be jealous when I have so much to live for? After all, aren't I the beloved?

DODIE: Yes you are, you are, and it hurts so bad.

RAINA: Good.

DODIE: No, not me. It's Allen. He's so, so sad. Not all the time. Not every minute. But it's there in the back of all the things he can't quite say to me, and all the ways we can't quite come together, and all the ways he keeps being brave. He's just so sad.

RAINA: What kind of man would he be if he weren't?

DODIE: And I love him. I do. Right down to my bones. I love him so much, it's breaking my heart.

RAINA: Fine. Then love him, love him and stop making trouble.

DODIE: I know, I know. But Raina, I'm so afraid.

RAINA: You should be. Love is a fearsome thing.

DODIE: I don't know . . . I don't know if I'm strong enough, to stay or to leave.

(Pause.)

What a pickle.

RAINA: He's a very loving man. You must trust me on this.

DODIE: He'll never love me the way he loved you.

RAINA: No. He'll love you the way he loves you. And that will be as much as you let him.

(Dodie nods. She takes a flower from the bouquet and hands it to Raina. Raina accepts it.)

DODIE: Yes. Thank you. Yes.

(The two women regard one another a moment, then Dodie turns and leaves. Raina inhales the flower's fragrance deeply.)

(Lights down.)

END OF PLAY

THE PLOT

Mark Troy

The Plot was first produced at the Baruch Performing Arts Center in New York City on December 10, 2005, as part of the Strawberry One Act Festival. *The Plot* was a finalist and winner of that week's competition. Cast: Colette Freedman — Effie; Diane Gale — Desdemona. The production was directed by Mark Troy.

CHARACTERS
DESDEMONA

EFFIE

SETTING
Effie's living room

●   ●   ●

The living room of Effie, thirties, sparsely decorated with two chairs and an end table with lamp. It's Canal Street. The doorbell rings and Effie shuffles in from her bedroom, depressed and tired. She has dark hair, deep features, and is in a stained bathrobe with her hair held up with a butterfly pin. She opens the door . . . and like a grandam, her mother, Desdemona, enters in Bergdorf Goodman dress, large-framed dark sunglasses, leather gloves, and a stylish scarf.

DESDEMONA: Darling, I am going to say this once and only once. You are never to make mention of it again. If I hear you make mention of it again, I am going to deny it, reject it, and pretend you have lost all senses of reality and I will disown you as your mother.
(Sits, folds her hand over her lap)
Don't you offer a guest coffee or a piece of danish when they come to your home?

EFFIE: If a guest came to my . . . OK, Mother.

DESDEMONA: Attitude. That's what you're famous for, my dear. But you are not going to give me attitude about this. This is something very serious.

EFFIE: *(Worried.)* Is it Dad?

DESDEMONA: I said serious — not irritating.

EFFIE: Fine, Mother.
(Effie exits.)

DESDEMONA: I'm telling you that father of yours is like a child. I treat him like a child. The other day he came in from the yard and his feet were covered in dirt. I sent him right to his room and for a shower. Oh he pouted and all, but I had to lay the law down. Do you have any idea what that new two-tone shag carpeting cost?
(Effie enters with a cup of coffee and a Danish.)

EFFIE: Are you going to tell me?

DESDEMONA: *(Without a beat.)* Twenty-five dollars a square foot!

EFFIE: A foot.

DESDEMONA: Twenty-five dollars a square foot, yes. I'm lucky it wasn't your father's foot squared, the man has feet like rhino. Woulda cost me a fortune. Anyway, that father of yours treats that carpet like it was a door mat. I tell you this — a doormat does not cost twenty-five dollars a square foot. What's this?

EFFIE: Coffee and a danish.

DESDEMONA: What am I supposed to do with it?

EFFIE: Mother. You said a good host would offer coffee and a danish.

DESDEMONA: Yes. But a good guest always says, "No thank you, don't bother on my account." Why didn't you ask?

EFFIE: Because I — Never mind.

(Effie shakes her head and exits.)

DESDEMONA: Darling, I am going to say this once and only once. Can you hear me in there?

EFFIE: *(Offstage.)* Even if I try not to.

DESDEMONA: You are never to make mention of it again. If I hear you make mention of it again, I am going to deny it, reject it, and pretend you were institutionalized for reasons only your doctor knows for sure. Do you want me to tell you this?

(Effie enters.)

EFFIE: Are you going to tell me this?

DESDEMONA: Caustic.

(Effie mouths the word "Caustic.")

DESDEMONA: — That's what you're famous for. But you're not going to be caustic about this. This is something very important.

(Effie sits, looks at her mother.)

EFFIE: So . . . what's the big issue?

DESDEMONA: Don't you offer a guest a pillow for their back?

EFFIE: If I had a guest . . . OK, Mother.

(Effie reluctantly exits.)

DESDEMONA: Your father isn't much of a host either, I'll tell you that, Effie. We once had a cocktail party for some of his business associates . . . or as I like to call them . . . "The boys from the shop who can't read or write." Anyway, that man, your father, didn't buy enough wine. There wasn't enough bread. The fish was cold. Cold fish. And halfway through he decided to do his imitation of Sammy Davis Jr. It was tasteless. Where he got the idea that covering his face with chocolate pudding would make the imitation more realistic, he makes me sick. The man makes me sick.

(Effie enters with a pillow poised to suffocate her mouth.)

EFFIE: M-M-M-M — mother?

DESDEMONA: *(Turns to her.)* Yes, dear?

EFFIE: *(Gently.)* Might I offer you a pillow for your back?

DESDEMONA: Am I some old lady? My back is fine. Now if you had something for the arthritis in my knee, then you'd be some daughter.

(Effie falls back on to the sofa and tries to suffocate herself with the pillow.)

EFFIE: So, no pillow.

DESDEMONA: No, pillow.

EFFIE: No pillow.

DESDEMONA: Aren't you going to offer your guest —

EFFIE: — No —

DESDEMONA: — Very well, darling. Then let's just get to it. I am going to say this once and only once. Do you promise never to bring it up again?

EFFIE: *(À la Groucho.)* Especially if I never hear it.

DESDEMONA: Your father and I went up to Mount Shalom in Medford. Exit Seventy-Four on the Long Island Expressway. If it was any further, the people there would be speaking Chinese. And don't get me started on what two hours in the car alone with your father is like.

EFFIE: What were you doing at the cemetery, Mother?

DESDEMONA: I was getting a tan — what do you think I was doing at the cemetery? OK, I'll say it. Your father and I bought plots.

EFFIE: I see. Well . . . you're both OK, right?

DESDEMONA: I'm fine, perfectly fine. If you're judging your father, physically he has the constitution of a zebra and can eat crap like others eat caviar. His mental state is another thing . . . yesterday I caught him drinking two bottles of Red Wine. He said something about not wanting to hear me complain about how he never puts the dishes in the dishwasher correctly, but I know it's because his boss wants to cut down his hours and it's upsetting him. Like it came out of left field. Do we really need men on the factory line getting more Cocoa Puffs to the markets putting in overtime? Your father thinks he's curing cancer. All he really does is give young children bad teeth.

EFFIE: Well you're both doing fine.

(Drinks the coffee she brought for her mother.)

I guess getting plots is the smart thing to do. It's very responsible of both of you.

DESDEMONA: Not for us, Effie, the plots are for you.

EFFIE: *(Spits the coffee out.)* For me?

DESDEMONA: You think your father is going to die? That man is going to live forever. Him and his drunken buddies who barely speak or write English.

But boy can they shove a small little plastic whistle into a box of cereal with class.

EFFIE: You bought me a cemetery plot?

DESDEMONA: We got a fabulous deal. If you die before you're eighty — we get free gardening for ten years.

EFFIE: That's terrible.

DESDEMONA: No. It cost a lot of money to keep up the grass and flowers in a place like Mount Shalom in Medford. I think it's worth it.

EFFIE: I'm not dying before I'm eighty!

DESDEMONA: Of course you're not, Effie. I'm just saying, if you did . . . we took the extra step of making sure you're not just sitting in dirt. You'll have tulips.

EFFIE: I don't like tulips.

DESDEMONA: I love tulips.

EFFIE: Why did you feel you needed to get me a funeral plot?

DESDEMONA: Because you're too irresponsible to do it yourself. Short-sighted — that's what you're famous for.

EFFIE: *(Losing patience.)* I'm thirty-two! Are you going to live my life for me?!

DESDEMONA: — You'll thank me for this, Effie. When you're lying there face up in the ground at Mount Shalom in Medford, in my favorite pink and green Oscar de la Renta gown, which is not as stained as that bathrobe you're always traipsing around in — you will thank me — and I will be on your mind.

EFFIE: That's my biggest nightmare.

DESDEMONA: It's never too early to think about the grim reaper, Effie. You were always like this. You didn't want to get your period either — but I told you it would happen. And sure enough . . .

EFFIE: — Yes, well you told me when I was five!

DESDEMONA: The point is . . . death comes to everyone and your father and I thought we would do this nice thing for you. Hey — you promised never to mention it again.

EFFIE: I've only just begun to mention it. No, Mother. This is serious.

DESDEMONA: But if I hear you make mention of it again, I am going to deny it, reject it and pretend you have deep seeded psychological problems from your father's brother Benjamin who to this day thinks he's the world famous athlete . . . Sea Biscuit.

EFFIE: I don't like the way this feels, Mother. The thought that there's a place for me . . . up there.

DESDEMONA: It's Medford. You love the Island.

EFFIE: Yes. For the food.

DESDEMONA: You'll be near Jack.

EFFIE: Jack?

DESDEMONA: Jackie.

(Gets emotional.)

My adopted greyhound I saved from the prison of South Florida where they raced her around the track chasing a rabbit like she was some animal.

EFFIE: Jackie Onasis was a dog.

DESDEMONA: Don't you talk that way about the president's wife!

EFFIE: I'm talking about the dog!

DESDEMONA: Well. If my little standard white poodle John was seen as my little president, I guess that does make my beloved greyhound Jackie — First-Dog.

EFFIE: This is not my life! This is a terrible life! I am not going to take this from you anymore, Mother. I hate you! You hear me? I HATE YOU! And I am not going to be buried in some plot at Mount Shalom in Medford in your sticking favorite pink and green Oscar de la Renta gown just so you can control me from the grave — it's not going to happen, it's not in the cards, you evil manipulative dominating, power-hungry old woman!!! I am worth more than that . . . I am more important than that — I demand a better life!!!

(Effie is about to cry as she crosses to the front door and faces it.)

DESDEMONA: *(Long pause.)* How can anyone speak of an Oscar de la Renta gown with such disdain? I've never been so disappointed in my own daughter, Effie.

EFFIE: *(Slow turn.)* Have you heard a single word I just —

DESDEMONA: — Anyway Jackie is buried just across the way from your plots. But if you peek between some trees, you can see her headstone. I got you matching ones. Jackie's has a picture of a little pooch on it. Yours I'm thinking will be a granite likeness of you in that stained bathrobe.

EFFIE: I'm near the pet cemetery?

DESDEMONA: Well it was either that or the view of the Long Island Expressway, and let's be honest, dear, you have such road rage.

EFFIE: Alright, fine. Let's not talk about this anymore.

DESDEMONA: I was asking for that.

(After a moment of silence.)

EFFIE: Can I get you some lunch?

DESDEMONA: Dear, you don't offer a guest lunch with your abilities in the kitchen. Are you trying to kill your own mother?

EFFIE: You are impossible!

DESDEMONA: I'm just being nice. And honest.

EFFIE: You're always correcting me, telling me what to do, how to do it. Never a pat on the back. Thirty-two and I feel I have never done anything to live up to your high standards. Maybe I should just kill you — this way you'll get out of my hair and be up up at Mount Shalom in Medford.

DESDEMONA: Oh I'm not being buried up in that hell hole, Effie.

EFFIE: You're not?

DESDEMONA: Your father and I like the city life. We have a mausoleum up on East 86th. Overlooking the park.

EFFIE: You're overlooking the park and I'm overlooking dogs and feline distemper victims?

DESDEMONA: Well you won't be alone.

EFFIE: I'm having company? But I'm a terrible host.

DESDEMONA: Effie. I'm going to say this once and only once. You should consider therapy.

EFFIE: Me? You! You should consider therapy.

DESDEMONA: First the pink gown, now this. It's a call for help, Effie. A call. Now your father and I have taken the necessary steps to secure buying you two plots.

EFFIE: Two plots?

DESDEMONA: For your husband. And you.

EFFIE: I'm not married.

DESDEMONA: You will.

EFFIE: I'm not dating.

DESDEMONA: You will.

EFFIE: I'm a lesbian.

DESDEMONA: They have cures.

EFFIE: I am not going through this with you again.

DESDEMONA: That's what I was asking for!

EFFIE: I cannot believe you would do this to me. Behind my back! You bought a plot for a person I haven't met yet!?

DESDEMONA: A MAN. A man you haven't met yet. Yes. This is just like the time I told you those breasts of yours would grow just like your grandmothers — she has to carry them around in supermarket basket — and I insisted we buy you a training bra.

EFFIE: When I was seven.

DESDEMONA: The point is I have always been prepared and I want you to be prepared for this.

EFFIE: For meeting a man I can be buried with.

DESDEMONA: Yes.

EFFIE: Even though I like girls.

DESDEMONA: I think you understand now. I might have just saved you money on your first therapy session.

EFFIE: So I'm supposed to tell a guy I just met that I already have a cemetery plot for him across the street from my mother's rescued greyhound?

DESDEMONA: Well don't bring it up on the first date of course, Effie, you wait. Maybe on your second date, you can pack a picnic basket and head out to Medford for a day in the sun.

EFFIE: — And nonchalantly spread out fried chicken and corn on the cob across the plots we're going to be buried in.

DESDEMONA: I thought we weren't going to talk about this?

EFFIE: You weren't going to talk about this, Mother, but I am going to talk about this. You crossed a line with this. You've been pushing your way into my life for years, but you've gone too far this time.

DESDEMONA: By doing such a nice thing?

EFFIE: By controlling!

DESDEMONA: You call it controlling. I call it love.

EFFIE: You won't even accept the fact that I'm gay.

DESDEMONA: I do accept that fact that you're gay. I also accept the fact that someday you'll be gay with a man.

EFFIE: I'm never going to get through to you!

DESDEMONA: Imagine how I feel?

EFFIE: I give up.

DESDEMONA: I'm not saying another word.

EFFIE: Good!

(Effie sits. Both women unable to communicate. Silence. Then . . .)

DESDEMONA: I don't think they allow two women to be buried in the same marital plot, Effie.

EFFIE: I probably won't ever meet anyone anyway. Look at me. I'm a mess.

DESDEMONA: You're not. You're just different. I always told your father you were different. You were like him. You were both very different. Oh my God — your father's a lesbian.

EFFIE: *(Laughs.)* I don't think so.

DESDEMONA: Eccentric. I call him eccentric. Especially when I'm not talking to him. I can call you eccentric if you'd like.

EFFIE: I hate my job. I can't meet anyone. I have a stained bathrobe. What's wrong with me, Mother?

DESDEMONA: Nothing that can't be turned around, Effie. You'll see. You'll turn this all around.

(More silence.)

EFFIE: You want to buy me something in the future, don't buy me a plot — buy me a blouse.

DESDEMONA: You know I can't do that, Effie. You have such terrible taste, how am I ever going to buy you something you like?

(Touches the robe.)

This won't come clean anymore, will it?

EFFIE: You talk about my attitude . . . what about your attitude? I'm the way I am because you're the way you are.

DESDEMONA: *(She has no comeback.)* I guess you are.

(They sit but can't look at each other. Long pause.)

DESDEMONA: I might have just saved you money on your second therapy session. So. Now that you know what's wrong with you, you can help yourself.

EFFIE: I just have to realize I shouldn't be like you in any way shape or form and I'll be fine.

DESDEMONA: Exactly.

(She realizes what she just said and cannot face Effie.)

EFFIE: Before I die, Mother . . . I would want us to be friends.

DESDEMONA: *(Softens.)* We're already friends, Effie.

(Off a look from Effie.)

OK, we can be better friends.

EFFIE: Thank you.

(They both nod.)

EFFIE: And I want you to be nicer to Dad.

DESDEMONA: You just want to hurt me, don't you?

(Off another look.)

Alright. Fine. I'll be nicer to the putz.

EFFIE: Thank you.

DESDEMONA: So . . . Is sex with dykes fulfilling?

EFFIE: You should probably leave now.

DESDEMONA: Good idea.

(Desdemona puts on her scarf and gloves.)

EFFIE: Thanks for coming by, Mother.

DESDEMONA: The plots are there if you want them, Effie. If you don't want them, maybe your children or . . . lesbians have children, don't they, Effie?

EFFIE: Good-bye, Mother.

(Desdemona puts on her sunglasses and crosses to the door.)

DESDEMONA: Darling, I am going to say this once and only once. You are never to make mention of it again. If I hear you make mention of it again, I am going to deny it, reject it, and pretend I am not your mother.

EFFIE: *(With a smile.)* Don't tempt me — just say it.

DESDEMONA: I'm proud you're my daughter.

(Effie is blown away.)

Yes. So you hate your job. Get a new job. You're smart enough. You can be anything you want to be. So you can't meet anyone. Go online. You never know . . . there a lot of pretty girls online, Effie. I see your lazy crackpot father looking at them all the time. But . . . I'm nice to him.

(Effie smiles.)

And as for that stained bathrobe. Well . . . it looks good on you.

(She turns to go, then back.)

DESDEMONA: Don't you offer a guest a kiss when they leave?

(Effie crosses to her and kisses her mom's cheek.)

DESDEMONA: You're a good hostess, Effie. Someday you're going to make someone a fabulous eccentric . . . husband?

(She tosses the scarf over her shoulder and exits. Effie thinks for a beat, then dials the phone.)

EFFIE: *(Into phone.)* Donna? It's Effie. From the gym. I'm in your spin class?

(Beat.)

Monday's Tuesday's Wednesday's Thursday's and Friday's.

(Beat.)

So, uhm, I was thinking . . . I mean, I'm not even sure you're a . . . lez . . . Maybe you and I can go out for a drink after a workout some time. You know. A drink, a smoke, it'll be good for us. Get the endorphins going.

(Realizes she's striking out.)

Maybe on our second date, I can pack a picnic basket and head out to Medford — I already have a cemetery plot for us across the street from my mother's rescued greyhound.

(No beat).

OK, Donna. I'll find a new spin class tomorrow.

(She hangs up . . . waves her arms madly at her mother. Gathers herself . . . dials again.)

EFFIE: Lisa? It's Effie . . . From Pilates . . .

(Slow fade to black.)

END OF PLAY

PRIZED BEGONIAS

BARA SWAIN

Original production: Playwrights Round Table, The Ninth Annual Summer Shorts Festival, *Laugh 'Til It Hurts* at Valencia Community College East Campus Black Box Theater, Orlando, Florida on July 27 to 28, 2006. Cast: Ms. Pink — Alaina Helliker; Ms. Black — Elizabeth Judith. Director: Bob Lipka. Artistic Director: Charles R. Dent.

CHARACTERS

Ms. Pink, Southerner; thirties to early fifties
Ms. Black, late twenties to late thirties

TIME

Present

SETTING

A cemetery

•   •   •

Setting: A cemetery. At Rise: Ms. Pink is sunning on a bench, face raised to the sky, eyes closed. She is wearing a pink sundress. The remnants of a bag lunch is next to her (clear baggy, pink grapefruit, and pink napkin). Ms. Black enters holding a bunch of pink flowers in her down-stretched hand. Trying not to disturb the sunning Ms. Pink, Ms. Black sits at the opposite end of the bench. She looks distracted. Ms. Black removes her black hat and places it next to her. Ms. Pink turns her head toward the intruder. She sits up and smiles apologetically.

MS. PINK: Warm day.

MS. BLACK: Yes.

MS. PINK: *(Indicating bouquet.)* Pretty flowers. Carnations?

MS. BLACK: Yes. I think so.

MS. PINK: Mmmm. Nice color.

(Ms. Black idly fingers the petals.)

MS. BLACK: My husband hates pink.

MS. PINK: Oh, my.

(Shrugs good-naturedly.)

Well, as long as he loves you.

MS. BLACK: That's true.

(Silence. Ms. Black folds her hands in her lap, holding her wedding band. Ms. Pink looks beyond her.)

MS. PINK: *(Affectionately.)* Oh, look! There's old Mrs. Weber.

(Pointing.)

Over there, by the three little flags. Mrs. Weber comes every first Sunday of the month to visit her grandson. He drowned during a fishing trip in 1977, just before Jimmy Carter was elected. Mrs. Weber says the only good thing that ever came out of Georgia was President Carter and

Cherokee roses. That's the state flower. They're white. The roses, I mean. Well, so is Jimmy Carter but all the presidents of the United States are white. White or dead.

(Sincerely.)

I hope I live to see the day when a Negro is elected president. Don't you?

MS. BLACK: I hadn't thought about it much.

MS. PINK: *(Gazing out again.)* Ohhh, look. Now, that's one handsome bunch of daffodils. I tried to grow some in a flower box last summer from some bulbs Mrs. Weber gave me? Well . . .

(Crossing her chest.)

. . . cross my heart, those poor yellow buds looked about as attractive as Delmonte's creamed corn. And the only thing less appealing than canned creamed corn, in my book, is canned creamed spinach.

(Shudders.)

Ooo. They both give me goose bumps.

(She suddenly brightens.)

'Scuse me.

(Ms. Pink rises. She waves to the distant Mrs. Weber and mouths: "Hi, Mrs. Weber. Nice flowers." She smiles broadly. "Thank you. You, too." Throwing little kisses and waving again. "Bye-bye!" Ms. Pink sits down.)

See how crooked she walks? Last year, Mrs. Weber had a second hip replacement. Her doctor was a Muslim. When her granddaughter had trouble with her first pregnancy, Mrs. Weber begged her to go to a Jewish doctor because if there's a choice . . . ?

(Confidentially.)

. . . they save the mother's life before they save the baby.

MS. BLACK: I didn't know that.

MS. PINK: Me either.

(She nods in another direction.)

Now, over there's the Bushwick plot. 1951–1995, 1949–1995. Poor Mr. and Mrs. Bushwick died in a car accident on the way to Coney Island.

(Pointing.)

And that's Sheila, the youngest daughter I believe. Her sister's as big as a house so it's hard to tell who's the oldest and, of course, I've never asked. My mama always says, "Double chins will double your age." But if you go like this, she says . . .

(She pats her chin with her left hand.)

. . . it helps.

(As she pats her chin, Ms. Pink invites Ms. Black to join her.)

MS. PINK: *(Continued.)* Go ahead. Try it.

(Encouraging.)

Go on.

MS. BLACK: Well, alright.

(Ms. Black joins her. The two women sit back, patting under their chins together in a peaceful silence.)

MS. PINK: Looks like Sheila bought some painted daisies again. My, aren't they tacky looking! Sheila buys whatever's on sale down the highway at the gas station, right next door to McDonald's? Her chubby sister is allergic to flowers but she's very close to God. She prays every other Sunday at her mama and daddy's grave with a double whopper, a large fries and a choco-late milkshake. Personally . . .

(She raises her eyebrows.)

. . . I prefer vanilla.

(Ms. Pink turns to face Ms. Black.)

Boy, this is hard work! My fingers are cramping. Shall we stop?

MS. BLACK: *(Smiling.)* Please, yes.

(They stop. Ms. Black shakes out her hand. Ms. Pink stretches her fingers. She turns to Ms. Black and extends her hand toward her.)

MS. PINK: Jesus, Mary and Joseph! I think my fingers have slimmed down some!

(Ms. Black laughs. Ms. Pink smiles and stretches back on the bench. They both gaze out in silence. Ms. Black speaks first.)

MS. BLACK: Are you paying your respects to someone, too?

MS. PINK: Oh, no. I'm just visiting. The grounds here are so beautiful? It kinda reminds me of home. Besides, I'm very attracted to the notion of perpet-ual care. Lord, I been taking care of myself for so long, the idea is very comforting. Very comforting. No, I'm just visiting . . .

(She crosses her fingers, hands and legs.)

. . . for now.

MS. BLACK: *(Confused.)* But aren't you married?

MS. PINK: Oh, you mean this?

(She raises her hand with a large wedding ring.)

Well, let me put it this way. You know how men always want what they can't have?

(Ms. Black nods.)

Well, the way I figure it is, if it looks like I'm already taken . . . ? I might just drum up a little interest.

MS. BLACK: Is it working?

MS. PINK: Hell, no. You see, the truth of the matter is, I'm not too smart. That's why Mama says to dress in bright clothes — to kinda throw everyone off track. I think I was born this way? But I tell all my male acquaintances that I was kicked in the head by a two-hundred-and-fifty-pound porker. Unless the male in question is also a two-hundred-and-fifty-pound porker, then I tell him it was a wild horse. It works most of the time. Except on Election Day. I don't believe I've ever gotten past first base on Election Day. Of course, any girl who's smart enough to hold a conversation with the male species on Election Day, I believe has the God-given right to get laid on Election Day.

(Wistfully.)

It's too bad, too. Because I'm very fond of politicians. Especially Democrats. They never wear matching socks! I find that very sexy. Very titillating. T.I.T.I.L.L.A.T.I.N.G. I can spell Poughkeepsie, New York, too, because my daddy almost got transferred there in 1971. But I like titillating better. It's got such a nice ring to it. Doesn't it?

MS. BLACK: Well, yes. It does.

MS. PINK: My cousin Billy, who's dyslexic and divorced twice, told me I was titillating in 1988. I was eating a pistachio ice-cream cone on Grandma Bitty's front porch and, Lord, I was dying to dig those nuts out of my back molars instead of charming my first cousin! Only I thought cousin Billy was diabetic and too henpecked, not dyslexic and two-timing his wife, so I was feeling kinda sorry for him. You know. Especially since I knew I'd just lay down and die if I couldn't have another lick of pistachio ice cream for the rest of my life, or worse yet, Breyer's vanilla with those little black specks that look like spider shit? So, to make a long story short, I let cousin Billy sweet-talk me into an uncompromising position that I was sure he couldn't, you know, complete, being a man of his affliction. ANYWAY, he could, we did, and I came this close to becoming his third wife except that I wanted children more than anything else in the world, even more than cousin Billy. And actually, I still do. Want children, I mean. More than anything.

(She sighs.)

Do you have any kids?

MS. BLACK: A little girl, yes.

MS. PINK: Ohhh, Lord. You're lucky. Especially if she looks like you.

MS. BLACK: Thank you. Actually, Lily favors her father.

MS. PINK: Lily. Is that your daughter's name? Lily?

MS. BLACK: Yes.

MS. PINK: Lily, Lily, Lily. That's one of my favorite flowers!

(She closes her eyes and sings.)

"A song of love is a sad song. Heigh Lily, heigh Lily, heigh lo."

(She smiles bashfully.)

There's some real pretty Lilies of the Valley near the main parking lot. They're hidden right behind the row of azalea bushes lining the sidewalk up to the Ladies Room? Sometimes I'm so taken by the sweet scent, I forget to empty my bladder!

(Shaking her head with pleasure.)

Mmm mmm. Did you catch a glimpse of those azaleas coming in?

MS. BLACK: *(Apologizing.)* I wasn't paying much attention.

MS. PINK: My Grandma Bitty from Arkansas . . . ? buried two dogs, a copy of Lassie Come Home and Grandpa Willie, right outside her kitchen window, smack in the middle of her favorite azalea bushes.

(Proudly.)

Some folk say she had the prettiest backyard west of the Mississippi! Two, three acres of wildflowers and a weeping willow that only cried at births and weddings, Grandpa Willie used to say. 'Though he never said much. And after his stroke? He never spoke again.

MS. BLACK: I'm sorry.

MS. PINK: It was a long time ago.

(Pensively.)

For the next two years, Grandma Bitty stayed by his side, tending to him like her prized begonias, fussing over him like a first-born. For two years she never set foot outside her own front door. But every evening, she'd slip out back and visit that old willow . . . wrap her arms around its trunk? . . . and whisper "knock knock" jokes.

MS. PINK: *(Continued.) (Tenderly.)* That willow never stopped weeping 'til the morning he died.

(Overwhelmed with emotion, she laughs.)

I rolled nineteen dollars worth of pennies the day Grandpa Willie got his wings! Poor Mama locked herself in the bedroom with a box of fig newtons and the family album. And Grandma Bitty? . . . she walked nine miles to town, joined Jack LaLane and the Democratic Club, and bought her first pair of panty hose.

(Passionately.)

She would've moved heaven and earth for that man. Ohhh, she loved him so.

(Ms. Pink swipes at her face, embarrassed by her display of emotion. Composed, she glances at Ms. Black who is silently weeping. Ms. Pink is concerned. Unsure of what to do, she leans toward the other grieving woman and speaks tentatively.)

MS. PINK: Knock knock.

(No answer. Ms. Pink tries again. She leans forward and raps loudly on the bench.)

Knock knock.

MS. BLACK: *(Reluctantly.)* Who's there.

MS. PINK: Boo.

MS. BLACK: *(Sniffing.)* Boo who?

MS. PINK: *(Gently.)* Why're you crying, pretty lady?

MS. BLACK: *(Weeping.)* I MISS MY HUSBAND.

> *(Ms. Pink reaches over to pat Ms. Black's hand.)*

MS. PINK: *(Softly.)* Of course you do. Of course you do.

> *(Ms. Black grasps her hand tightly in hers. Ms. Pink shifts over next to her. Ms. Black rests her head against Ms. Pink's shoulder.)*

It's alright. Everything's gonna be alright.

> *(Ms. Pink plants kisses on the top of her head. She rocks Ms. Black gently and sings.)*

MS. PINK: *(Singing.)* "A song of love is a sad song. Heigh Lily, Heigh Lily, Heigh Lo. Hmm hmm hmm hmm hmm hmm hmm hmm hmm. Don't ask me how I know."

> *(Ms. Pink continues humming softly as the lights dim out.)*

END OF PLAY

PUMPKIN PATCH

PATRICK GABRIDGE

Pumpkin Patch premiered May 28, 2007, at the New York
Fifteen-Minute Play Festival, produced by the American Globe
and Turnip Theatre Companies, at the American Globe
Theatre. John Basil, Gloria Falzer, and Liz Keefe, producers.
Directed by Halina Ujda. Cast: LaToya — Keisha Zollar;
Sasha — Helen McElwain.

CHARACTERS
> LaToya, a black woman, thirties to forties
> Sasha, a white woman, thirties to forties

SETTING
> A community garden in an urban neighborhood, rich with tall plants, pumpkin vines, and three pumpkins.

• • •

A community garden, rich with tall plants and pumpkin vines and three pumpkins. A black woman in her thirties to forties, Latoya, stands up, with a plastic shopping bag of vegetables dangling from her wrist and hefts up a large pumpkin. A white woman in a garden hat, Sasha, also in her thirties to forties, carries a shovel, walks up the path toward Latoya.

SASHA: Hi.

LATOYA: Hello.

SASHA: Beautiful day.

LATOYA: Gorgeous.

SASHA: This is my favorite time of year in the garden. Everything so ripe.

LATOYA: Gem of the neighborhood.

SASHA: I'm glad you think so. *(Beat.)* Can I help you?

LATOYA: I've got it, thanks.

SASHA: I didn't actually mean it like that.

LATOYA: If you could just move out of my way.

SASHA: What I meant was, who are you and what are you doing?

LATOYA: I'm just taking my pumpkin.

SASHA: It's a beauty.

LATOYA: Finest pumpkin I've ever seen.

SASHA: I think so, too. But that's not your pumpkin.

LATOYA: Sure it is. See, look, it's in my arms. And it's heavy, so if you'll excuse me.

> *(Latoya tries to get past Sasha, but she won't budge.)*

SASHA: Put it down please.

LATOYA: Look, Lady, get the hell out of my way.

SASHA: I'm the coordinator for this community garden. I know all the gardeners, and I don't know you.

LATOYA: I'm just picking some stuff for my cousin. He's out of town.

SASHA: Right. Of course. What's your cousin's name?

LATOYA: Uh. William.

SASHA: William doesn't have a plot here this year. Jerry planted the pumpkin patch.

LATOYA: That's who I meant. Cousin Jerry.

SASHA: We've been having a problem with people stealing produce out of the gardens.

(Latoya's arms are getting tired. She sets down the pumpkin.)

LATOYA: It's a community garden. I'm part of the community. I've been part of the community a lot longer than you. You all move in and think you own the neighborhood.

SASHA: I've been here long enough.

LATOYA: Yeah, well, I used to have a plot here, years ago, after it used to be just rubble from a building somebody torched. My aunt helped make this place.

SASHA: But you don't have a plot here now.

LATOYA: Look, it's just one pumpkin.

SASHA: Plus a bag full of . . .

LATOYA: A couple tomatoes. Look at those plots. There's fruit all over the ground, just going to waste. They're not taking care of them either, look at all those weeds. I thought maybe they were abandoned.

SASHA: And the eggplant?

LATOYA: Nobody needs that much eggplant. And they're beauties.

SASHA: They're Lester's beauties. Not yours. We work hard to grow these vegetables. We dig, weed, water. You've done nothing.

LATOYA: I'd like a plot, but money's tight.

SASHA: The plot fee is only twenty-five dollars, but we can work something out. Sign up for a plot next year, and you can grow whatever you want.

LATOYA: I don't have time.

SASHA: Put the vegetables back.

LATOYA: They're picked now anyway. If I put them down, they're just gonna rot.

SASHA: You can't have them.

LATOYA: You want them?

SASHA: I grew my own.

LATOYA: No sense wasting these. I'll just take them with me.

(Sasha pulls a cell phone out of her pocket.)

SASHA: Look, either you leave without the vegetables, or I'll call the police.

LATOYA: For what?

SASHA: Theft. It's against the law to take something that doesn't belong to you.

LATOYA: You'd have me go to jail for picking a couple tomatoes?

SASHA: And an eggplant. And a pumpkin. Which you did not grow, or even ask permission to take. It's not just the tomatoes and pumpkins. Someone dug up my echinacea right out of my plot. Someone else took Tanya's rudbeckia. The gardens get raided every season, and I've had enough.

LATOYA: You want to make an example of me, so you call your attack dogs.

SASHA: The police.

LATOYA: What do you care? I'm just an ignorant black woman. Plenty of us in jail already. What's one more, right?

SASHA: Just don't take the vegetables.

LATOYA: And if I do, you think the right solution is to lock me up, make me lose my job, my apartment, get kicked out on the street? For a couple tomatoes that were gonna fall on the ground and rot?

SASHA: I am not the person doing the wrong thing here. Look, you can have some tomatoes. I'll give you some from my own plot. But you have to leave the pumpkin.

LATOYA: Hell no. Go ahead. Call the police. You can't prove it's not my pumpkin. There's no receipts out here. I say it's mine, you say it's not.

SASHA: Who do you think the cops will believe?

LATOYA: Oh, I know who they'll believe. You got all the race cards right in your pocket, don't you?

SASHA: It's not your pumpkin. Don't you get it? Jerry planted that abandoned plot, watered the vines, fertilized them, picked off the beetles. All summer long. There used to be a dozen. And now we've only got three left. I told him he'd get his heart broken. Every year, I tell the gardeners, don't grow watermelons, don't grow pumpkins, or don't grow anything that will disappear. But he planted them anyway.

LATOYA: He should have listened to you. 'Cause you know what it's like around here. You know what we're like, what I'm like. You've got us pegged. All us black folks is thieves. Make sure you lock your house up tight at night, missy. You tell Jerry to lock up against those Negroes.

SASHA: Jerry's black.

LATOYA: Then you tell Jerry that a sister needed one of his pumpkins to make a little pie.

SASHA: Tell you what. I'll call him and ask him to come down here, so you can request permission to take his pumpkin.

LATOYA: I don't think so.

(Latoya picks up the pumpkin again.)

LATOYA: *(Continued.)* I need to go. Get out of my way.

SASHA: Put the pumpkin down.

LATOYA: It's my pumpkin now.

SASHA: It's not your pumpkin

(Latoya approaches Sasha, who grabs her shovel tighter.)

LATOYA: Don't even think about raising that shovel at me.

SASHA: Put down the pumpkin.

LATOYA: Touch me with that shovel, and you'll be looking for your teeth all over this garden.

SASHA: Thief.

LATOYA: Move.

SASHA: Thief!

(Latoya pushes past Sasha, who drops the shovel and grabs the pumpkin.)

LATOYA: Don't touch me.

SASHA: Give me that.

LATOYA: Let go.

SASHA: That is not your pumpkin.

(They tussle. Sasha ends up with the pumpkin.)

SASHA: *(Continued.)* Get out of my garden.

LATOYA: Give me my pumpkin.

SASHA: You want your pumpkin. Here's your pumpkin.

(Sasha raises the pumpkin high overhead and smashes it down on the ground. She tramples the broken pieces into the earth.)

SASHA: *(Continued.)* You. Can't. Have. It.

LATOYA: Crazy bitch.

(Sasha picks up the shovel.)

SASHA: Crazy? You want to see crazy?

(Sasha goes to the pumpkin vine and smashes the other pumpkins.)

LATOYA: Lady. Lady. Stop! I won't take any more. All right. Hey. Hey. Calm down.

SASHA: I told him not to plant pumpkins. I told them not to grow watermelons. But they call me every week and whine over the phone, "someone keeps stealing my fruit." Plant green beans, I tell them. No one ever steals green beans. Plant zucchini, you can't even give them away in August. But don't plan melons. Don't plant pumpkins. DON'T PLANT PUMPKINS!

(Sasha finishes smashing all the pumpkins and looks out at vines, breathing hard.)

LATOYA: Nobody gonna steal no pumpkins today.

SASHA: That's right.

LATOYA: Nobody gonna have no pumpkins.

SASHA: That's right.

LATOYA: Not even Jerry.

SASHA: Idiot.

LATOYA: Not you, not me, not Jerry. No pumpkins.

SASHA: Shut up.

LATOYA: Problem solved.

SASHA: It's all your fault.

LATOYA: That's right. We all know who's to blame.

   (Latoya picks up her bag of tomatoes and eggplant.)

SASHA: Get out of my garden.

LATOYA: It's a community garden.

SASHA: And leave those tomatoes.

LATOYA: Want to smash these, too?

   (Latoya starts to toss the vegetables at Sasha's feet.)

SASHA: Shut up.

LATOYA: Plow it all under, lady. Plow it all under. Otherwise someone who needs a carrot might just help himself. Someone who admires a squash might take it home. And that's gonna hurt. Plow it all under.

   (Latoya exits.)

   (Sasha looks around at the destruction she's caused.)

   (Lights to black.)

END OF PLAY

STOP RAIN

Patrick Gabridge

Stop Rain premiered at the Boston Theatre Marathon, May 21, 2006, produced by the Underground Railway Theatre, at the Wimberly Theatre/Boston Center for the Arts, Calderwood Pavilion. Boston Theatre Marathon Artistic Director: Kate Snodgrass. Directed by Judith Braha. Cast: Marla — Debra Wise; Rain — Eliza Fichter.

CHARACTERS
    MARLA, a woman in her thirties to forties.
    RAIN, a young woman, eighteen to twenty-four.

PLACE
    A park bench

TIME
    The present

• • •

Scene: A park bench. At Rise: Marla waits impatiently. She's in her late thirties and wears a business suit. Finally, Rain enters, a little anxious. She's in her late teens or early twenties, shabbily dressed.

RAIN: Sorry.

MARLA: I've been waiting more than an hour.

RAIN: The buses are all screwed up. I hate the bus. The people smell, the men press up against you. And you always gotta wait for the damn thing. Waiting's not my thing, you know.

MARLA: Mine neither.

RAIN: Right. Sorry. You look nice. Is that a new suit?

MARLA: No. It's just one I wear to work. I had to take off from work to be here.

RAIN: Right. It looks good. I know you're busy and all that . . . I've been looking for a job.

MARLA: I thought you had one. At the grocery store.

RAIN: Didn't work out. My manager, he was crazy. Always making remarks, you know, passes. I like to flirt a little sometimes, but he . . . You know how it is. And the buses suck. I had to take two transfers to get there.

MARLA: What happened to the car?

RAIN: The car.

MARLA: The car, Rain. The money. The car that Rich helped you choose, so it would be reliable. So you could keep a job.

RAIN: Right. About the car. That's sort of why I called you.

MARLA: Did it break down?

RAIN: Not exactly.

MARLA: Julio.

RAIN: He said he was going to the store for some bread and milk, just like a normal person. Then I don't see him for two days, and when he comes dragging his sorry ass home, no car. Not even most of the money left. You should have heard me scream at him. I kicked him out that night.

MARLA: But he's back.

RAIN: Some things you can't explain.

MARLA: No.

RAIN: So the car was really a good idea, Marla. I learned my lesson. If I had another, I'd hide the keys. You know I hate to ask for anything, but you know what they say about the poor man: Give him a fish and he eats today, teach him to fish and he, you know, eats a lot more.

MARLA: Aren't you even going to ask about him?

RAIN: You know I want to . . . How's Nathan?

MARLA: He's great. I brought some pictures.

(She pulls out an envelope and sets it on the bench next to Rain, who looks at it, but doesn't pick it up.)

RAIN: Thanks. What's he doing these days?

MARLA: The whole pre-school thing. He likes the social part of it, making new friends, the playground. When he comes home, he's full of stories of who did this and who did that. He's even starting to read a few words — *dog, cat. Stop, go.* It's like a window opened up to his mind, and all of a sudden *a,b,c, go dog go.* He's amazing.

RAIN: You're a good . . . a good mother to him now. And I'm sure Rich is a good father.

MARLA: We're trying. It's not always easy, but we're very happy. And grateful, Rain. We'll always be grateful to you.

RAIN: It was the right choice for me. For him. I'm glad it was you that adopted him.

MARLA: Rain?

RAIN: Hmm.

MARLA: You missed our meeting last week.

RAIN: I didn't forget. Don't let him think I forgot. I . . . it was the car and Julio and the buses and I . . .

MARLA: You should have called.

RAIN: My phone's out. If I can get a job again —

MARLA: You should have found a pay phone, something.

RAIN: I guess I could have left a message, but . . . Was Nathan pretty disappointed?

MARLA: Of course he was. This is the third time this year, Rain. It's one thing to let us down, we're grown-ups, we can handle it. He's just a little boy.

RAIN: I won't let it happen again.

MARLA: Neither will we.

RAIN: What do you mean?

MARLA: Rich and I have been talking. Debating. Arguing. It doesn't need to be permanent. It would be good for him to know you, to have a connection to his roots. The books all say he'll need it. But for now, he's too young to be so deeply disappointed so often.

RAIN: You're cutting me off?

MARLA: We want to suspend visits, yes. For a while. We'll keep sending pictures and letters, and we still want them from you.

RAIN: He's my son.

MARLA: And he's my son, too.

RAIN: I gave him life.

MARLA: We know that. All three of us want you to be a part of his life. You're the one who acts like you don't.

RAIN: That's a lie. Sometimes I screw up. I'll make it right.

MARLA: He's only four, Rain. He shouldn't have to do this.

RAIN: But he does, because I'm his mother and that's the way I am.

MARLA: Oh, you've proved it to him quite well. It's hard for him to understand any of this, and the way you've behaved will just make him angry with you.

RAIN: It's an angry world, Marla. I'll do better, I promise. I do a lot of stupid things in my life. I know that. But most days, I know I did the right thing by giving him to you and Rich. But at night, sometimes I wake up and think about him, about him being with me, snuggled in bed, curled up in a little ball in my arms, and I stroke his hair to calm him after his nightmare and I wrap my arms around him. Blood of my blood, breath of my breath. I hold him tight, so he knows he's safe and I'll never let him go. Sometimes I'll stay like that all night, with him in my arms and in my mind, more than a dream, more than a dream. Until the sun comes up, and I have to let him go back to you and Rich, let him go all over again. It hurts, deep in my guts, and I know it won't ever go away. All I want to do is lay there in bed, all day long, until the darkness comes again, and I can have him back.

MARLA: You can't have him back.

RAIN: I know you're a good mother to him. I know it. But even a bad mother, like me, wants to see her son.

MARLA: We all want the same thing, right? For Nathan to grow up safe and happy and loved. Don't make him doubt that he's worthy of being loved.

RAIN: I missed a few meetings, that's all . . . I can find you. I have your phone number. I figured out your last name. I know people with computers, and they say that's all it takes. I can find where you live.

MARLA: Is that a threat?

RAIN: It's a fact.

MARLA: And what then? You want to take four years of building trust and flush it down the toilet?

RAIN: You're the one who suddenly wants to change things.

MARLA: Because you're hurting him.

RAIN: It was an accident.

MARLA: But you know what, that's fine. If you want to undo all that, go ahead. Make yourself the bad guy.

RAIN: Of course, it has to be me. Look at you, you have everything — a house, a job, an education, a husband. And now you have a son. How am I supposed to fit in with all that? I'm stupid and messy. My life is out of control. But I exist. You can't pretend I don't. Nathan knows better.

MARLA: We give you chance after chance, but you keep blowing it. We opened our lives to you.

RAIN: Give me a fucking break. We met a few times, in out-of-the-way places, places I can hardly get to. You saw how completely whacked my world is, and you felt guilty, so you paid me off a little. But I fuck up a few times, and you slam the door in my face. That mess is why you have a son. You've been looking for an excuse, Marla. Opened your lives to me? I gave you my son. You gave me a few hours of your time, gave me a couple breaks. I just want a scrap, a few hours with Nathan, every once in a while. You're a mother now. What does that mean to you?

MARLA: I . . . I know what it means.

RAIN: Fine. You're in control. You decide. OK? But you have to let me keep trying. Please? One more chance?

MARLA: I promised Rich that I would not waver. Let me talk to him, OK?

RAIN: OK.

MARLA: But try to do something right. Send Nathan a letter.

RAIN: I will. I'll send a whole handful.

MARLA: I'm sorry.

RAIN: Don't be. I'm going to take care of it. You'll see.

MARLA: I have to go back to work.

RAIN: Yeah . . . Hug him for me. Please? I mean, really think of me when you're doing it. I'll know.

MARLA: I will.

(There's an awkward moment of parting, a consideration of an embrace, but it doesn't happen. Marla exits.)

STOP RAIN • 227

(Rain picks up the envelope and opens it. She examines each photo slowly, touching the faces, trying to keep her composure. She hunts in her ragged purse for a pen and a scrap of paper and begins to write as: Lights to black.)

END OF PLAY

THE THERAPEUTIC HOUR

Guy Fredrick Glass

Original Production: First performed on February 21, 2007, in the Hackensack Theater and Playwright Festival, The Hackensack Cultural Arts Center, Hackensack, New Jersey. Cast: Dorothy — Hannah Snyder-Beck; Cassie — Nanci Cone; Waitress — Jennifer Sandella. Director: Sara Lampert Hoover. Producer: Ciona Taylor Productions.

CHARACTERS

CASSIE, thirties, overweight, insecure
DOROTHY, twenties, beautiful, self-centered

TIME AND PLACE

A café. The present.

•   •   •

At rise, Cassie is sitting at a table in a café, pointing at her watch. Dorothy has just entered. She stands by the table.

CASSIE: It's exactly two forty-five. I wasn't sure you'd come.

DOROTHY: I'm here, aren't I?

(Dorothy sits.)

CASSIE: Still, I wasn't sure you'd come. You had no obligation.

DOROTHY: This was my time. I have nowhere else to be at this hour.

CASSIE: He was always punctual. I loved that about him. Among other things. He gave me so much. And now he's gone . . . What did you say your name was?

DOROTHY: I didn't say. I'm Dorothy.

CASSIE: Really?

DOROTHY: Yes.

CASSIE: That wasn't my name for you. I imagined your name was Isabella. Something evocative. Something foreign. I imagined he favored you because you were foreign . . . Are you foreign?

DOROTHY: No. I'm from Connecticut.

CASSIE: What did you imagine about me?

DOROTHY: I never imagined anything about you.

CASSIE: Nothing?

DOROTHY: No. You were the woman who came out of the room at exactly two forty-five. Nothing more and nothing less.

CASSIE: My name is Cassie . . . Didn't you ever wonder what my name was?

DOROTHY: No. Sorry. I never did. Should I have?

CASSIE: He told me it was normal to wonder about you. I was . . . am envious of your figure. You've got a beautiful body.

DOROTHY: Thank you. I don't know what to say . . . Uh, shall I order us some coffee?

CASSIE: I've already had a latte . . . and a piece of Boston cream pie. They're kind of famous for it here. I've been sitting down since two o'clock. *(With disappointment.)* I promised him I wouldn't eat sweets. He said it was a poor substitute for love. I wanted to look like you. Isabella.

DOROTHY: Dorothy.

(She tries to get the waitress' attention.)

Miss? Miss?

CASSIE: But what does it matter now?

DOROTHY: I understand. Two o'clock was your time. You needed to have something . . . to give you some gratification. For the therapeutic hour. I understand.

CASSIE: To give me some gratification . . .

DOROTHY: *(To the waitress.)* A cup of coffee. Black. No. Nothing else.

CASSIE: . . . or for spite. Won't you have a piece of pie?

DOROTHY: No. Thank you . . . Didn't you promise him you wouldn't eat sweets?

CASSIE: *(To the waitress.)* Bring me another slice of Boston cream. And two forks . . . *(Looking at Dorothy.)* . . . just in case.

DOROTHY: I've got something I need to get off my chest.

CASSIE: Oh?

DOROTHY: You're the last connection I have to him. Cassie. The only one who knows about two forty-five. Never sent in a claim form. Always paid in cash. No trace of our relationship . . . Our *therapeutic* relationship.

CASSIE: We filled out a treatment plan every six sessions. I'm with an HMO. Guess I gave him a lot of trouble. I had a chart on me that's an inch thick.

DOROTHY: *Some* patients can well afford to pay in cash. He never took notes. There should be no trace.

CASSIE: No notes? Mine was the thickest chart in his file cabinet. He had to start a second folder. That's how I know he loved me. Did you ever see my chart on his desk when you came into the room? It was the big thick one. You might have seen it. Maybe you didn't know what it was.

DOROTHY: I don't remember seeing your chart, Cassie. I don't remember seeing any charts.

CASSIE: He was so professional. He wouldn't have left it on the desk for you to see. He must have put it in his briefcase. He had an expensive-looking suede briefcase. Chocolate brown. *(She titters nervously.)* Like my pie. He must have put it in his briefcase. He told me I was so complex. He probably needed to bring me home to study. My appointments were only forty-five minutes long. But he must have spent hours a day thinking about me.

DOROTHY: I'm sure he did. But I've got something I need to get off my chest. It's about him. And me.

CASSIE: You weren't his favorite patient. I was. You need to know that right off the bat. You need to admit that to me. We had a special relationship, him and me. I was in his briefcase, in a manner of speaking. He took me home with him at night.

DOROTHY: I'm sure it was very special.

(Pause.)

CASSIE: I'm not sure I like your attitude, Isabella.

DOROTHY: Dorothy.

CASSIE: There's something very patronizing about your tone of voice. Something smug and patronizing.

DOROTHY: I have hardly said a thing. I wanted to. But maybe now I won't.

CASSIE: If you've got something to say about you and him it may be something I don't want to hear.

DOROTHY: I thought you would understand. I thought you would be the only one who would understand. But I may have been wrong.

(She takes money out and begins to get up to leave.)

Here. I don't need a cup of coffee. I'll go.

CASSIE: No. Please sit down.

(Dorothy sits down again.)

DOROTHY: If you're sure it's not too painful. The suddenness of it . . . is a shock to us all.

CASSIE: It is a shock. And the way I found out about it . . . was a shock.

DOROTHY: What do you mean?

CASSIE: The obituary . . . in the newspaper. That his middle name was "George." That he was Jewish. That he had a wife and a seven-year-old daughter. I didn't know those things. I didn't want to know those things. I would have thought I'd be the first one to know . . . about his death. That they would have called me first. I had the thickest chart by far. We filled out treatment plans every six sessions. He said I was complex.

DOROTHY: We are nobody. We don't exist.

CASSIE: I exist. With my out-of-shape figure, I exist. With my chart that is bulging at the seams, I exist.

DOROTHY: We were like shadows in his life, Cassie. There and not there.

CASSIE: I shared my secrets with him. Did he have a secret pain that he kept from me, from us, for months? For years? Was he suffering silently in that stuffed armchair with a secret pain? I could have consoled him. It would have brought us closer. I would have understood. I have a secret pain. Why didn't he trust me with his?

DOROTHY: We sat in the back row of the chapel. Nameless. You and I. And a dozen other bewildered faces. In a pew with ripped upholstery. As if some misguided lover had taken her pocket knife, in her grief, and plunged it into the wrong place.

CASSIE: No one would even say how he died. It was like they all knew. Except me.

DOROTHY: The service. In a language I could not understand.

CASSIE: I fantasized you could understand. I fantasized you were foreign.

DOROTHY: Then I waited my turn to file past the casket.

CASSIE: You looked elegant and simple in your mourning clothes. You know, you always do.

DOROTHY: Wanting to get one last look at him.

CASSIE: No one wants to look at me. Look at me.

DOROTHY: A woman in black — was it his wife? — stared at me full in the face.

CASSIE: I receded into the background so that no one could see me. I always do.

DOROTHY: As if she could see into the recesses of my heart. As if she knew . . .
(Pause.)

CASSIE: Knew *what?*

DOROTHY: Cassie.

CASSIE: What is it? You can tell me anything.

DOROTHY: I . . .

CASSIE: You said you had something you wanted to get off your chest.

DOROTHY: I don't want to hurt you.

CASSIE: You said you thought I'd be the only one who would understand.

DOROTHY: Don't make me say anything to hurt you.

CASSIE: I left that couch nice and warm for you. Five days a week. It was nice and warm by the time I left at two forty-five.

DOROTHY: Why don't I take you up on your kind offer.
(Dorothy reaches for the pie.)

CASSIE: I want to know what happened in that room at two fifty.

DOROTHY: Why don't you pass me the pie . . . and a fork.

CASSIE: . . . at two fifty-seven . . .

DOROTHY: Just a forkful or two. This stuff destroys your figure.

CASSIE: . . . at three oh one . . .

DOROTHY: Why tarnish your memory of him, Cassie. Yours was the thickest chart in the file cabinet. You had a special relationship.
(Cassie passes the plate and a fork to Dorothy.)

CASSIE: I want to know what was happening in that room at three oh eight.

DOROTHY: He brought you home at night, in a manner of speaking. No one can take that away from you.

(Dorothy takes a forkful of pie.)

CASSIE: I want to know why his wife stared you full in the face.

DOROTHY: No one can ever take that away . . . Say, this pie is delicious.

CASSIE: Stop talking about the pie!

DOROTHY: I just may have another slice. *(To the waitress.)* Miss? Miss?

CASSIE: God damn it. Look at me.

DOROTHY: *(To the waitress.)* Will you bring us another slice of Boston cream?
(To Cassie.) I can see why they're so famous for it here.

CASSIE: You never even wondered what my name was.

DOROTHY: They do a nice job with the pie . . . And the coffee's not bad either.

CASSIE: You never imagined anything about me?

DOROTHY: No. Sorry. I never did. Should I have?

CASSIE: Dorothy.

DOROTHY: Cassie.

CASSIE: There is something I want to ask . . .

DOROTHY: I'm not sure . . .

CASSIE: You. There is something I need to know.

DOROTHY: . . . I want to go there.

CASSIE: Something that makes all the difference in the world.

DOROTHY: No. This is *my* time. Two forty-five. *My* hour. *My* . . . therapeutic
hour.

CASSIE: So it is.

DOROTHY: You spent your hour eating pie and drinking latte, before I got here.

CASSIE: So I did . . . I needed to have something to give me some gratification.

DOROTHY: And there is something I want to ask *you* . . . Cassie. *(Beat.)* Did
you kill him?

CASSIE: I . . .

DOROTHY: I want to know what was happening in that room at two
eleven . . .

CASSIE: My life is nothing. I have no money. I have no friends. I have nothing.

DOROTHY: . . . At two twenty-three . . .

CASSIE: I spent my sessions fantasizing about you. You are so beautiful . . .

DOROTHY: . . . At two thirty-six . . .

CASSIE: My name for you was Isabella. Isn't that a beautiful name?

DOROTHY: I want to know what was happening in that room at two forty-two.

CASSIE: I killed him because I fantasized he was having an affair with you.

DOROTHY: So you *did* kill him.

CASSIE: No. But I wish I had. How could he choose you over me?

DOROTHY: Choose . . . me . . .

CASSIE: *Wasn't* he having an affair with you?

DOROTHY: *(Hesitatingly.)* Of course not. *(Beat.)* Wasn't he the consummate professional?

(Cassie looks at her watch.)

CASSIE: It's three thirty.

DOROTHY: Is it? That means my time is up.

(Dorothy begins to get up to leave. Cassie remains seated.)

CASSIE: I'm glad you came. You had no obligation.

DOROTHY: This was my time. I have nowhere else to be at this hour.

CASSIE: Where will you be tomorrow? At two forty-five?

DOROTHY: Here. With you. Where else do I have to go?

(Blackout.)

END OF PLAY

THE VAN BUREN CLOAK ROOM

ADAM KRAAR

The Van Buren Cloak Room was first produced at the H.B. Playwrights Foundation & Theatre in June, 2005. It was directed by Randy White with the following cast: Roz — Tamilla Woodard; Ellen — Patricia Randell.

CHARACTERS

ROZ, twenty-five, African-American, a Secret Service agent. A person of deep conviction. Proud, efficient, curious, and somewhat eccentric.

ELLEN, thirty-something, white, a book reviewer. Intense, witty, and mercurial; somewhat dotty and meshuga; a humanist.

PLACE

The White House

TIME

The present

• • •

An odd room in the White House. It is small and windowless. On the wall is an old, bad oil painting, a portrait of a puffed-up turkey. There is a wooden chair and a coat rack. At Rise, Roz stands facing Ellen. Roz, twenty-five, African-American, is dressed in a Secret Service uniform. Ellen, thirty-something, white, wears a coat, pants, and a stylish blouse.

ELLEN: I demand to know: What is going on?

ROZ: Your coat, ma'am.

ELLEN: What is this place?

ROZ: This is the Van Buren Cloak Room.

ELLEN: Van Buren . . . ?

ROZ: Prior to that, during the Adams administration, it was the plucking room.

ELLEN: Uh huh.

ROZ: It was in this room that the White House poultry master would pluck the birds that were to be consumed by the president, his family and his guests.

ELLEN: Are you planning to pluck me?

ROZ: No, ma'am. Not if you take off your coat.
  (Roz receives a communication over her earpiece, and replies, talking into her sleeve.)

ROZ: Yes, sir. We're in the V.B. Room. . . . Yes, sir. Including — ? . . . Right.

ELLEN: Excuse me. Where's my cousin? Are you holding her too? . . . Look, she's from the suburbs. She wrote her Congressman to get this stupid — . . . this tour.
  Why am I here? This is America. I still have rights. Don't I?

ROZ: Yes, ma'am.

(Beat.)

ELLEN: . . . My name is Ellen, Ellen Rosenfeld.

(Ellen extends her hand.)

ROZ: Agent Rosalind Lincoln. I cannot shake your hand until I complete the pat down.

ELLEN: This is . . . outrageous!

(Roz takes down a coat hanger.)

ELLEN: W-w-what are you doing?

ROZ: For your coat.

ELLEN: Oh.

(Relieved:)

Oh!

ROZ: You'll notice the embossed Presidential seal on this hanger. It was originally manufactured by the Big Top Department Store for the first inauguration of Dwight D. Eisenhower.

(Slight pause.)

Your coat?

ELLEN: OK; OK: enough is enough. I will not hang my conscience on an Eisenhower coat hanger. My feathers may be blue — a proud, blue-state sblue — but I am not your turkey!

(Roz gives Ellen a stern look. Ellen takes off her coat, accepts the hanger, and hangs it up.)

ELLEN: Bet this coat rack was manufactured by Halliburton.

ROZ: Please put your feet on those marks, and extend your arms like this.

ELLEN: Absurd! . . . Look. On the floor. A feather!

(After a moment, Roz picks up the feather and examines it. She looks suspiciously at Ellen for a long moment — did Ellen plant this feather here, or did someone else? — then Roz puts the feather in her coat pocket.)

ROZ: Your feet.

ELLEN: I should warn you —

ROZ: Anything sharp concealed on your person?

ELLEN: I'm extremely ticklish. One time at the airport I made an entire security platoon collapse in hysterics. Flights were delayed for hours.

ROZ: Secret Service trains much better than that. We spend a whole semester on the principles of frisking.

(Indicates spreading:)

Arms.

(Ellen spreads her arms.)

ELLEN: *(Warning her:)* Gonna crack up—

(Roz takes out a tongue depressor and gives it to Ellen.)

ROZ: It may help you to bite down on this.

ELLEN: What is this? A tongue depressor from the Polk administration?

ROZ: Just do it!

(Ellen bites down on the tongue depressor. Roz begins the pat down. Ellen giggles occasionally, emitting strange, anarchic squeals.)

ROZ: I am now going to pat your chest area.

(Roz continues the pat down. Ellen explodes with wild laughter. Roz is infected and starts to laugh herself. Ellen takes out the tongue depressor, and the two women share a good laugh. Roz abruptly stops laughing, stands up straight, puts her finger to her ear and then talks into her sleeve.)

ROZ: — Sir? . . . I'm doing it right now. . . . There's been some resistance—

ELLEN: I'm not resisting!

ROZ: *(Somewhat defensively:)* . . . I can handle it. . . . That won't happen, sir. Yes sir, I'm sure. . . . Right away.

ELLEN: Is that Rumsfeld, playing with his ham radio?

ROZ: *(With a new intensity:)* This is a very serious matter. I advise you not to make jokes. They could be used against you.

ELLEN: *(Becoming worried:)* What did that guy say? I mean, we're really just here for the tour. I swear! — Is this about my mother?

ROZ: What about your mother?

ELLEN: I knew it! Listen, no one reads her magazine except burnt-out vegans and alien abductees — she's harmless! And I have nothing to do with her. She's ashamed of me. She thinks what I do is not "socially significant."

ROZ: What is it you do?

ELLEN: I'm a book reviewer, for *Vogue. Vogue* magazine.

ROZ: I know *Vogue.*

ELLEN: My day job. I'm also a member of the United Negro College Fund. One in four African-American males is in trouble with the law, and what is your guy doing about it? Jack.

ROZ: Arms out, please.

ELLEN: Just tell me one thing. As an African-American, aren't you — ?

ROZ: I'm not going to ask you again.

ELLEN: What about Condeleeza's hair? Where is your outrage?!

(Roz aggressively pushes Ellen against the wall.)

ROZ: *(With urgency:)* Hands up on the wall. Now!

(Ellen puts her hands up against the wall. Roz pushes Ellen into position and completes the pat down. Ellen, terrified, becomes very quiet and still.)

ROZ: . . . Ms. Rosenfeld.

ELLEN: What?!

(She turns to look.)

ROZ: *(Indicating chair:)* Please.

(Pause. Ellen sits down.)

ROZ: Did you know in advance that the president was going to be passing by the Map Room?

ELLEN: No. I never dreamed we'd have to see him.

ROZ: Did you say, when you were inside the Map Room . . .

(Taking out a piece of paper for reference:)

"God, I'd like to slap that smug, smirking face of his"?

ELLEN: Is that what this is about?

ROZ: Did you say that?

ELLEN: What if I did? I mean, don't you, don't you find that smirk insufferable?

ROZ: That's just the way his face —

ELLEN: Oh come on. That smirk, that chuckle —

(Imitates:) "heh heh heh" — that vacant look in his eyes, as he proclaims he's on a mission from God. — Oh no . . . You think he's on a mission from God?

ROZ: I think we're all on a mission from God.

ELLEN: *("Now I'm really in trouble!")* Oh, God!!

ROZ: We just have to quiet down a bit and hear what He has to tell us.

ELLEN: *(To herself:)* This is the worst year of my entire life.

(To Roz; extremely vulnerable:)

What's gonna happen to me?

ROZ: Just . . . answer my questions. Alright?

ELLEN: *(Trying to explain her behavior:)* It's just — I couldn't believe they re-elected him, that's all. Do you have any idea what's going to happen to us — to this planet? I think I may have a little tumor on my ear, because this nut — this president — thinks the ozone layer can be replaced with Astroturf.

ROZ: You sure it's not just a freckle?

ELLEN: I don't know! I don't know.

ROZ: May I take a look?

ELLEN: . . . OK.

ROZ: . . . Doesn't look like anything to me. You could easily get it checked out.

ELLEN: I could. I could. . . . Do you know it is impossible to find a good man in New York City? I mean, literally impossible. So you compromise, bit by bit, till you end up . . .

ROZ: End up . . . ?

ELLEN: I . . . I don't know who I am anymore. Yeah. . . . I thought I was part of this vital cultural force, that all the crap I was enduring was leading to something important and noble — like . . . The March on Washington — or Chekhov's short stories, or two brilliant children, with cheeks like . . .

ROZ: Mm.

ELLEN: — Something way beyond reviewing glorified beach books and hand-cuffing my boyfriend to the radiator — Ever since the election, it's the only way he can — never mind. . . . I don't know what's going on anymore. Do you?

ROZ: . . . Sometimes I come here on my break, just to . . . just to listen to the sounds of this House.

ELLEN: Yeah?

ROZ: And sometimes I think I can hear Abraham Lincoln, sighing and then prayin'.

(Beat.)

I really shouldn't be —

ELLEN: No! Go on. Please.

ROZ: Sometimes . . . I hear Franklin Roosevelt. His stomach made strange noises — like he had the whole country in there. He prayed too, but kept it a secret. And then, sometimes, I hear, well, I hear the turkeys. I hear 'em clucking and gobbling and makin' a fuss. I think a lot of turkeys must've come through here.

ELLEN: *(A wisecrack:)* You're telling me.

(Beat. Then, sincerely:) That feather. You think it was . . . ?

ROZ: Could be. Could very well be.

(A moment. Then Roz gets a communication over her earpiece.)

ROZ: *(Speaking into her sleeve:)* Sir? Yes. She's clean. . . . I interrogated her and — . . . Are you sure that's necessary? . . . What exactly — ? . . . Yes, sir.

(Pause: Roz is perturbed.)

ELLEN: What?

ROZ: My supervisor is saying they found a flyer on your cousin, which could be interpreted —

ELLEN: We got those from some college kids — There's nothing illegal about a flyer showing W with a butt face. . . . Right?

ROZ: No. But I've been ordered to strip-search you.

ELLEN: *(Standing up:)* You're kidding!

ROZ: Those are my orders. . . . I'm already on report —

ELLEN: On report? Why??

ROZ: We need to —

ELLEN: Come on!

(Beat.)

They pardon turkeys, don't they? Every Thanksgiving, one turkey is let off the hook — it's the American way, right?

(Pause.)

ROZ: My grandfather was a White House chef for forty-one years, and my father worked in the kitchen too. I first visited this place when I was four years old. Got to shake President Reagan's hand. . . . Then, on the way home, my father told me, he told me how he'd once gotten arrested for marching. Just for marching.

(Pause.)

You wouldn't really slap the president, would you?

ELLEN: . . . No. My mother would've slapped him. — But she's in Vermont. I only talk to her once a month.

ROZ: Here's what we're gonna do. (God, I hope I'm doing the right thing here.) — We're going to act as if I strip-searched you. Alright? Muss up your sweater a little bit. But if you say anything to anyone, I'm going to be very disappointed in you.

ELLEN: I won't. Thank you. You — . . . You're a good American.

(Suddenly smelling something:)

. . . What's that . . .

ROZ: From the kitchen — Turkey gumbo. Recipe goes back to the Kennedy administration. After the visit of Nikita Khrushchev, they had forty gallons of it frozen and shipped to the Kremlin.

ELLEN: Your grandfather's recipe?

(Roz nods. Ellen looks at her with awe. Roz straightens up her uniform. Ellen musses up her sweater to make it look like she was strip-searched.)

(Lights fade to black.)

END OF PLAY

RIGHTS AND PERMISSIONS